The Importance of
Being Earnest

with Connections

The Importance of Being Earnest

Oscar Wilde

with
Connections

HOLT, RINEHART AND WINSTON
Harcourt Brace & Company
Austin • New York • Orlando • Atlanta • San Francisco
Boston • Dallas • Toronto • London

For permission to reprint copyrighted material, grateful acknowledgment is made to the following sources:

Susan Bergholz Literary Services, New York: "And Some More" and "My Name" from *The House on Mango Street* by Sandra Cisneros. Copyright © 1984 by Sandra Cisneros. Published by Vintage Books, a division of Random House, Inc., and in hardcover by Alfred A. Knopf in 1994. All rights reserved. **Buffalo Bill Memorial Association:** from "Oscar Wilde Goes West" by Margaret Malkind from *The American West,* vol. XVIII, no. 1, January/February 1981. Copyright © 1981 by the American West Publishing Company. **Crown Publishers, Inc.:** "Taking the Manly Way Out" from *Dave Barry Talks Back* by Dave Barry. Copyright © 1991 by Dave Barry. **Doubleday, a division of Random House, Inc.:** From "The Endless Streetcar Ride into the Night, and the Tinfoil Noose" from *In God We Trust, All Others Pay Cash* by Jean Shepherd. Copyright © 1966 by Jean Shepherd. **Harcourt Brace & Company:** "The Naming of Cats" from *Old Possum's Book of Practical Cats* by T. S. Eliot. Copyright 1930 by T. S. Eliot; copyright renewed © 1967 by Esme Valerie Eliot. **Macmillan General Reference USA, a division of Ahsuog, Inc.:** From definitions "Benvenuto Cellini," "Brahmin," "Chippendale," "Limoges," and "Majolica" adapted from *Webster's New World Dictionary of American English, Third College Edition* by Editor-in-Chief, Victoria Neufeldt and Editor-in Chief Emeritus, David B. Guralnik. Copyright © 1988 by Macmillan. **Simon & Schuster, Inc.:** "For Anne Gregory" from *The Poems of W. B. Yeats: A New Edition,* edited by Richard J. Finneran. Copyright 1933 by Macmillan Publishing Company and copyright renewed © 1961 by Bertha Georgie Yeats.

Cover: HRW photo by Scott Van Osdol

Contents

The Persons of the Play

John Worthing, J.P.
Algernon Moncrieff
Rev. Canon Chasuble, D.D.
Merriman, Butler
Lane, Manservant
Lady Bracknell
Hon. Gwendolen Fairfax
Cecily Cardew
Miss Prism, Governess

The Scenes of the Play

Act I
Morning-room in Algernon Moncrieff's flat in
Half-Moon Street, W.
Act II
The Garden at the Manor House, Woolton
Act III
Drawing-Room at the Manor House, Woolton

ACT ONE

Scene: Morning-room in ALGERNON's *flat in Half-Moon Street. The room is luxuriously and artistically furnished. The sound of a piano is heard in the adjoining room.*

(LANE *is arranging afternoon tea on the table, and after the music has ceased,* ALGERNON *enters.*)

Algernon. Did you hear what I was playing, Lane?

Lane. I didn't think it polite to listen, sir.

Algernon. I'm sorry for that, for your sake. I don't play accurately—anyone can play accurately—but I play with wonderful expression. As far as the piano is concerned, sentiment is my forte. I keep science for Life.

Lane. Yes, sir.

Algernon. And, speaking of the science of Life, have you got the cucumber sandwiches cut for Lady Bracknell?

Lane. Yes, sir. (*Hands them on a salver.*)

Algernon. (*Inspects them, takes two, and sits down on the sofa.*) Oh! . . . by the way, Lane, I see from your book that on Thursday night, when Lord Shoreman and Mr.

1

Worthing were dining with me, eight bottles of champagne are entered as having been consumed.

Lane. Yes, sir; eight bottles and a pint.

Algernon. Why is it that at a bachelor's establishment the servants invariably drink the champagne? I ask merely for information.

Lane. I attribute it to the superior quality of the wine, sir. I have often observed that in married households the champagne is rarely of a first-rate brand.

Algernon. Good heavens! Is marriage so demoralizing as that?

Lane. I believe it *is* a very pleasant state, sir. I have had very little experience of it myself up to the present. I have only been married once. That was in consequence of a misunderstanding between myself and a young person.

Algernon. (*Languidly.*) I don't know that I am much interested in your family life, Lane.

Lane. No, sir; it is not a very interesting subject. I never think of it myself.

Algernon. Very natural, I am sure. That will do, Lane, thank you.

Lane. Thank you, sir.

(LANE *goes out.*)

Algernon. Lane's views on marriage seem somewhat lax. Really, if the lower orders don't set us a good example, what on earth is the use of them? They seem, as a class, to have absolutely no sense of moral responsibility.

(Enter LANE.*)*

Lane. Mr. Ernest Worthing.

(Enter JACK. LANE *goes out.)*

Algernon. How are you, my dear Ernest? What brings you up to town?

Jack. Oh, pleasure, pleasure! What else should bring one anywhere? Eating as usual, I see, Algy!

Algernon. *(Stiffly.)* I believe it is customary in good society to take some slight refreshment at five o'clock. Where have you been since last Thursday?

Jack. *(Sitting down on the sofa.)* In the country.

Algernon. What on earth do you do there?

Jack. *(Pulling off his gloves.)* When one is in town one amuses oneself. When one is in the country one amuses other people. It is excessively boring.

Algernon. And who are the people you amuse?

Jack. *(Airily.)* Oh, neighbors, neighbours.

Algernon. Got nice neighbors in your part of Shropshire?

Jack. Perfectly horrid! Never speak to one of them.

Algernon. How immensely you must amuse them! *(Goes over and takes sandwich.)* By the way, Shropshire is your county, is it not?

Jack. Eh? Shropshire? Yes, of course. Hallo! Why all these cups? Why cucumber sandwiches? Why such reckless extravagance in one so young? Who is coming to tea?

Algernon. Oh! merely Aunt Augusta and Gwendolen.

Jack. How perfectly delightful!

Algernon. Yes, that is all very well; but I am afraid Aunt Augusta won't quite approve of your being here.

Jack. May I ask why?

Algernon. My dear fellow, the way you flirt with Gwendolen is perfectly disgraceful. It is almost as bad as the way Gwendolen flirts with you.

Jack. I am in love with Gwendolen. I have come up to town expressly to propose to her.

Algernon. I thought you had come up for pleasure? . . . I call that business.

Jack. How utterly unromantic you are!

Algernon. I really don't see anything romantic in proposing. It is very romantic to be in love. But there is nothing romantic about a definite proposal. Why, one may be accepted. One usually is, I believe. Then the excitement is all over. The very essence of romance is uncertainty. If ever I get married, I'll certainly try to forget the fact.

Jack. I have no doubt about that, dear Algy. The Divorce Court was specially invented for people whose memories are so curiously constituted.

Algernon. Oh! there is no use speculating on that subject. Divorces are made in Heaven—(JACK *puts out his hand to take a sandwich.* ALGERNON *at once interferes.*) Please don't touch the cucumber sandwiches. They are ordered specially for Aunt Augusta. (*Takes one and eats it.*)

Jack. Well, you have been eating them all the time.

Algernon. That is quite a different matter. She is my aunt. (*Takes plate from below.*) Have some bread and butter. The bread and butter is for Gwendolen. Gwendolen is devoted to bread and butter.

Jack. (*Advancing to table and helping himself.*) And very good bread and butter it is too.

Algernon. Well, my dear fellow, you need not eat as if you were going to eat it all. You behave as if you were married to her already. You are not married to her already, and I don't think you ever will be.

Jack. Why on earth do you say that?

Algernon. Well, in the first place girls never marry the men they flirt with. Girls don't think it right.

Jack. Oh, that is nonsense!

Algernon. It isn't. It is a great truth. It accounts for the extraordinary number of bachelors that one sees all over the place. In the second place, I don't give my consent.

Jack. Your consent!

Algernon. My dear fellow, Gwendolen is my first cousin. And before I allow you to marry her, you will have to clear up the whole question of Cecily. (*Rings bell.*)

Jack. Cecily! What on earth do you mean? What do you mean, Algy, by Cecily! I don't know anyone of the name of Cecily.

(*Enter* LANE.)

Algernon. Bring me that cigarette case Mr. Worthing left in the smoking-room the last time he dined here.

Lane. Yes, sir.

(LANE goes out.)

Jack. Do you mean to say you have had my cigarette case all this time? I wish to goodness you had let me know. I have been writing frantic letters to Scotland Yard about it. I was very nearly offering a large reward.

Algernon. Well, I wish you would offer one. I happen to be more than usually hard up.

Jack. There is no good offering a large reward now that the thing is found.

(Enter LANE with the cigarette case on a salver. ALGERNON takes it at once. LANE goes out.)

Algernon. I think that is rather mean of you, Ernest, I must say. *(Opens case and examines it.)* However, it makes no matter, for, now that I look at the inscription inside, I find that the thing isn't yours after all.

Jack. Of course it's mine. *(Moving to him.)* You have seen me with it a hundred times, and you have no right whatsoever to read what is written inside. It is a very ungentlemanly thing to read a private cigarette case.

Algernon. Oh! it is absurd to have a hard and fast rule about what one should read and what one shouldn't. More than half of modern culture depends on what one shouldn't read.

Jack. I am quite aware of the fact, and I don't propose to discuss modern culture. It isn't the sort of thing one should talk of in private. I simply want my cigarette case back.

Algernon. Yes; but this isn't your cigarette case. This cigarette case is a present from someone of the name of Cecily, and you said you didn't know anyone of that name.

Jack. Well, if you want to know, Cecily happens to be my aunt.

Algernon. Your aunt!

Jack. Yes. Charming old lady she is, too. Lives at Tunbridge Wells. Just give it back to me, Algy.

Algernon. (*Retreating to back of sofa.*) But why does she call herself Cecily if she is your aunt and lives at Tunbridge Wells? (*Reading.*) "From little Cecily with her fondest love."

Jack. (*Moving to sofa and kneeling upon it.*) My dear fellow, what on earth is there in that? Some aunts are tall, some aunts are not tall. That is a matter that surely an aunt may be allowed to decide for herself. You seem to think that every aunt should be exactly like your aunt! That is absurd! For Heaven's sake give me back my cigarette case. (*Follows* ALGERNON *round the room.*)

Algernon. Yes. But why does your aunt call you her uncle? "From little Cecily, with her fondest love to her dear Uncle Jack." There is no objection, I admit, to an aunt being a small aunt, but why an aunt, no matter what her size may be, should call her own nephew her uncle, I can't quite make out. Besides, your name isn't Jack at all; it is Ernest.

Jack. It isn't Ernest; it's Jack.

Algernon. You have always told me it was Ernest. I have introduced you to everyone as Ernest. You answer to the name of Ernest. You look as if your name was Ernest. You are the most earnest-looking person I ever saw in my life. It is perfectly absurd your saying that your name isn't Ernest. It's on your cards. Here is one of them. (*Taking it from case.*) "Mr. Ernest Worthing, B.4, The Albany." I'll keep this as a proof that your name is Ernest if ever you attempt to deny it to me, or to Gwendolen, or to anyone else. (*Puts the card in his pocket.*)

Jack. Well, my name is Ernest in town and Jack in the country, and the cigarette case was given to me in the country.

Algernon. Yes, but that does not account for the fact that your small Aunt Cecily, who lives at Tunbridge Wells, calls you her dear uncle. Come, old boy, you had much better have the thing out at once.

Jack. My dear Algy, you talk exactly as if you were a dentist. It is very vulgar to talk like a dentist when one isn't a dentist. It produces a false impression.

Algernon. Well, that is exactly what dentists always do. Now, go on! Tell me the whole thing. I may mention that I have always suspected you of being a confirmed and secret Bunburyist; and I am quite sure of it now.

Jack. Bunburyist? What on earth do you mean by a Bunburyist?

Algernon. I'll reveal to you the meaning of that incomparable expression as soon as you are kind enough to inform me why you are Ernest in town and Jack in the country.

Jack. Well, produce my cigarette case first.

Algernon. Here it is. (*Hands cigarette case.*) Now produce your explanation, and pray make it improbable. (*Sits on sofa.*)

Jack. My dear fellow, there is nothing improbable about my explanation at all. In fact, it's perfectly ordinary. Old Mr. Thomas Cardew, who adopted me when I was a little boy, made me in his will guardian to his granddaughter, Miss Cecily Cardew. Cecily, who addresses me as her uncle from motives of respect that you could not possibly appreciate, lives at my place in the country under the charge of her admirable governess, Miss Prism.

Algernon. Where is that place in the country, by the way?

Jack. That is nothing to you, dear boy. You are not going to be invited. . . . I may tell you candidly that the place is not in Shropshire.

Algernon. I suspected that, my dear fellow! I have Bunburyed all over Shropshire on two separate occasions. Now, go on. Why are you Ernest in town and Jack in the country?

Jack. My dear Algy, I don't know whether you will be able to understand my real motives. You are hardly serious enough. When one is placed in the position of guardian, one has to adopt a very high moral tone on all subjects. It's one's duty to do so. And as a high moral tone can hardly be said to conduce very much to either one's health or one's happiness, in order to get up to town I have always pretended to have a younger brother of the name of Ernest, who lives in the Albany, and gets into the most dreadful scrapes. That, my dear Algy, is the whole truth pure and simple.

Algernon. The truth is rarely pure and never simple. Modern life would be very tedious if it were either, and modern literature a complete impossibility!

Jack. That wouldn't be at all a bad thing.

Algernon. Literary criticism is not your forte, my dear fellow. Don't try it. You should leave that to people who haven't been at a University. They do it so well in the daily papers. What you really are is a Bunburyist. I was quite right in saying you were a Bunburyist. You are one of the most advanced Bunburyists I know.

Jack. What on earth do you mean?

Algernon. You have invented a very useful younger brother called Ernest, in order that you may be able to come up to town as often as you like. I have invented an invaluable permanent invalid called Bunbury, in order that I may be able to go down into the country whenever I choose. Bunbury is perfectly invaluable. If it wasn't for Bunbury's extraordinary bad health, for instance, I wouldn't be able to dine with you at Willis's tonight, for I have been really engaged to Aunt Augusta for more than a week.

Jack. I haven't asked you to dine with me anywhere tonight.

Algernon. I know. You are absurdly careless about sending out invitations. It is very foolish of you. Nothing annoys people so much as not receiving invitations.

Jack. You had much better dine with your Aunt Augusta.

Algernon. I haven't the smallest intention of doing anything of the kind. To begin with, I dined there on Monday, and once a week is quite enough to dine with one's own relations. In the second place, whenever I do dine there I am always treated as a member of the family, and sent down with either no woman at all, or two. In the third place, I know perfectly well whom she will place me next to, tonight. She will place me next Mary Farquhar, who always flirts with her own husband across the dinner-table. That is not very pleasant. Indeed, it is not even decent . . . and that sort of thing is enormously on the increase. The amount of women in London who flirt with their own husbands is perfectly scandalous. It looks so bad. It is simply washing one's clean linen in public. Besides, now that I know you to be a confirmed Bunburyist, I naturally want to talk to you about Bunburying. I want to tell you the rules.

Jack. I'm not a Bunburyist at all. If Gwendolen accepts me, I am going to kill my brother, indeed I think I'll kill him in any case. Cecily is a little too much interested in him. It is rather a bore. So I am going to get rid of Ernest. And I strongly advise you to do the same with Mr. . . . with your invalid friend who has the absurd name.

Algernon. Nothing will induce me to part with Bunbury, and if you ever get married, which seems to me extremely problematic, you will be very glad to know Bunbury. A man who marries without knowing Bunbury has a very tedious time of it.

Jack. That is nonsense. If I marry a charming girl like Gwendolen, and she is the only girl I ever saw in my life that I would marry, I certainly won't want to know Bunbury.

Algernon. Then your wife will. You don't seem to realize, that in married life three is company and two is none.

Jack. (*Sententiously.*) That, my dear young friend, is the theory that the corrupt French Drama has been propounding for the last fifty years.

Algernon. Yes; and that the happy English home has proved in half the time.

Jack. For heaven's sake, don't try to be cynical. It's perfectly easy to be cynical.

Algernon. My dear fellow, it isn't easy to be anything nowadays. There's such a lot of beastly competition about. (*The sound of an electric bell is heard.*) Ah! that must be Aunt Augusta. Only relatives, or creditors, ever ring in that Wagnerian manner. Now, if I get her out of the way for ten minutes, so that you can have an opportunity for proposing to Gwendolen, may I dine with you tonight at Willis's?

Jack. I suppose so, if you want to.

Algernon. Yes, but you must be serious about it. I hate people who are not serious about meals. It is so shallow of them.

(*Enter* LANE.)

Lane. Lady Bracknell and Miss Fairfax.

(ALGERNON *goes forward to meet them. Enter*
LADY BRACKNELL *and* GWENDOLEN.)

Lady Bracknell. Good afternoon, dear Algernon, I hope you are behaving very well.

Algernon. I'm feeling very well, Aunt Augusta.

Lady Bracknell. That's not quite the same thing. In fact the two things rarely go together. (*Sees* JACK *and bows to him with icy coldness.*)

Algernon. (*To* GWENDOLEN.) Dear me, you are smart!

Gwendolen. I am always smart! Am I not, Mr. Worthing?

Jack. You're quite perfect, Miss Fairfax.

Gwendolen. Oh! I hope I am not that. It would leave no room for developments, and I intend to develop in many directions.

(GWENDOLEN *and* JACK *sit down together in the corner.*)

Lady Bracknell. I'm sorry if we are a little late, Algernon, but I was obliged to call on dear Lady Harbury. I hadn't been there since her poor husband's death. I never saw a woman so altered; she looks quite twenty years younger. And now I'll have a cup of tea, and one of those nice cucumber sandwiches you promised me.

Algernon. Certainly, Aunt Augusta. (*Goes over to teatable.*)

Lady Bracknell. Won't you come and sit here, Gwendolen?

Gwendolen. Thanks, mamma, I'm quite comfortable where I am.

Algernon. (*Picking up empty plate in horror.*) Good

heavens! Lane! Why are there no cucumber sandwiches? I ordered them specially.

Lane. (*Gravely.*) There were no cucumbers in the market this morning, sir. I went down twice.

Algernon. No cucumbers!

Lane. No, sir. Not even for ready money.

Algernon. That will do, Lane, thank you.

Lane. Thank you, sir. (*Goes out.*)

Algernon. I am greatly distressed, Aunt Augusta, about there being no cucumbers, not even for ready money.

Lady Bracknell. It really makes no matter, Algernon. I had some crumpets with Lady Harbury, who seems to me to be living entirely for pleasure now.

Algernon. I hear her hair has turned quite gold from grief.

Lady Bracknell. It certainly has changed its color. From what cause I, of course, cannot say. (ALGERNON *crosses and hands tea.*) Thank you. I've quite a treat for you tonight, Algernon. I am going to send you down with Mary Farquhar. She is such a nice woman, and so attentive to her husband. It's delightful to watch them.

Algernon. I am afraid, Aunt Augusta, I shall have to give up the pleasure of dining with you tonight after all.

Lady Bracknell. (*Frowning.*) I hope not, Algernon. It would put my table completely out. Your uncle would have to dine upstairs. Fortunately he is accustomed to that.

Algernon. It is a great bore, and, I need hardly say, a terrible disappointment to me, but the fact is I have just had a telegram to say that my poor friend Bunbury is very ill again. (*Exchanges glances with* JACK.) They seem to think I should be with him.

Lady Bracknell. It is very strange. This Mr. Bunbury seems to suffer from curiously bad health.

Algernon. Yes; poor Bunbury is a dreadful invalid.

Lady Bracknell. Well, I must say, Algernon, that I think it is high time that Mr. Bunbury made up his mind whether he was going to live or to die. This shilly-shallying with the question is absurd. Nor do I in any way approve of the modern sympathy with invalids. I consider it morbid. Illness of any kind is hardly a thing to be encouraged in others. Health is the primary duty of life. I am always telling that to your poor uncle, but he never seems to take much notice . . . as far as any improvement in his ailment goes. I should be obliged if you would ask Mr. Bunbury, from me, to be kind enough not to have a relapse on Saturday, for I rely on you to arrange my music for me. It is my last reception, and one wants something that will encourage conversation, particularly at the end of the season when everyone has practically said whatever they had to say, which, in most cases, was probably not much.

Algernon. I'll speak to Bunbury, Aunt Augusta, if he is still conscious, and I think I can promise you he'll be all right by Saturday. Of course the music is a great difficulty. You see, if one plays good music, people don't listen, and if one plays bad music people don't talk. But I'll run over the program I've drawn out, if you will kindly come into the next room for a moment.

Lady Bracknell. Thank you, Algernon. It is very thoughtful of you. (*Rising, and following* ALGERNON.) I'm sure the program will be delightful, after a few expurgations. French songs I cannot possibly allow. People always seem to think that they are improper, and either look shocked, which is vulgar, or laugh, which is worse. But German sounds a thoroughly respectable language, and, indeed I believe it is so. Gwendolen, you will accompany me.

Gwendolen. Certainly, mamma.

(LADY BRACKNELL *and* ALGERNON *go into the music-room,* GWENDOLEN *remains behind.*)

Jack. Charming day it has been, Miss Fairfax.

Gwendolen. Pray don't talk to me about the weather, Mr. Worthing. Whenever people talk to me about the weather, I always feel quite certain that they mean something else. And that makes me so nervous.

Jack. I do mean something else.

Gwendolen. I thought so. In fact, I am never wrong.

Jack. And I would like to be allowed to take advantage of Lady Bracknell's temporary absence. . . .

Gwendolen. I would certainly advise you to do so. Mamma has a way of coming back suddenly into a room that I have often had to speak to her about.

Jack. (*Nervously.*) Miss Fairfax, ever since I met you I have admired you more than any girl . . . I have ever met since . . . I met you.

Gwendolen. Yes, I am quite aware of the fact. And I

often wish that in public, at any rate, you had been more demonstrative. For me you have always had an irresistible fascination. Even before I met you I was far from indifferent to you. (JACK *looks at her in amazement.*) We live, as I hope you know, Mr. Worthing, in an age of ideals. The fact is constantly mentioned in the more expensive monthly magazines, and has reached the provincial pulpits I am told; and my ideal has always been to love someone of the name of Ernest. There is something in that name that inspires absolute confidence. The moment Algernon first mentioned to me that he had a friend called Ernest, I knew I was destined to love you.

Jack. You really love me, Gwendolen?

Gwendolen. Passionately!

Jack. Darling! You don't know how happy you've made me.

Gwendolen. My own Ernest!

Jack. But you don't really mean to say that you couldn't love me if my name wasn't Ernest?

Gwendolen. But your name is Ernest.

Jack. Yes, I know it is. But supposing it was something else? Do you mean to say you couldn't love me then?

Gwendolen. (*Glibly.*) Ah! that is clearly a metaphysical speculation, and like most metaphysical speculations has very little reference at all to the actual facts of real life, as we know them.

Jack. Personally, darling, to speak quite candidly, I don't much care about the name of Ernest . . . I don't think the name suits me at all.

Gwendolen. It suits you perfectly. It is a divine name. It has a music of its own. It produces vibrations.

Jack. Well, really, Gwendolen, I must say that I think there are lots of other much nicer names. I think Jack, for instance, a charming name.

Gwendolen. Jack? . . . No, there is very little music in the name Jack, if any at all, indeed. It does not thrill. It produces absolutely no vibrations. . . . I have known several Jacks, and they all, without exception, were more than usually plain. Besides, Jack is a notorious domesticity for John! And I pity any woman who is married to a man called John. She would probably never be allowed to know the entrancing pleasure of a single moment's solitude. The only really safe name is Ernest.

Jack. Gwendolen, I must get christened at once—I mean we must get married at once. There is no time to be lost.

Gwendolen. Married, Mr. Worthing?

Jack. (*Astounded.*) Well . . . surely. You know that I love you, and you led me to believe, Miss Fairfax, that you were not absolutely indifferent to me.

Gwendolen. I adore you. But you haven't proposed to me yet. Nothing has been said at all about marriage. The subject has not even been touched on.

Jack. Well . . . may I propose to you now?

Gwendolen. I think it would be an admirable opportunity. And to spare you any possible disappointment, Mr. Worthing, I think it only fair to tell you quite frankly beforehand that I am fully determined to accept you.

Jack. Gwendolen!

Gwendolen. Yes, Mr. Worthing, what have you got to say to me?

Jack. You know what I have got to say to you.

Gwendolen. Yes, but you don't say it.

Jack. Gwendolen, will you marry me? (*Goes on his knees.*)

Gwendolen. Of course I will, darling. How long you have been about it! I am afraid you have had very little experience in how to propose.

Jack. My own one, I have never loved anyone in the world but you.

Gwendolen. Yes, but men often propose for practice. I know my brother Gerald does. All my girl-friends tell me so. What wonderfully blue eyes you have, Ernest! They are quite, quite blue. I hope you will always look at me just like that, especially when there are other people present.

(Enter LADY BRACKNELL.)

Lady Bracknell. Mr. Worthing! Rise, sir, from this semi-recumbent posture. It is most indecorous.

Gwendolen. Mamma! (*He tries to rise; she restrains him.*) I must beg you to retire. This is no place for you. Besides, Mr. Worthing has not quite finished yet.

Lady Bracknell. Finished what, may I ask?

Gwendolen. I am engaged to Mr. Worthing, Mamma. (*They rise together.*)

Lady Bracknell. Pardon me, you are not engaged to

anyone. When you do become engaged to someone, I, or your father, should his health permit him, will inform you of the fact. An engagement should come on a young girl as a surprise, pleasant or unpleasant, as the case may be. It is hardly a matter that she could be allowed to arrange for herself. . . . And now I have a few questions to put to you, Mr. Worthing. While I am making these inquiries, you, Gwendolen, will wait for me below in the carriage.

Gwendolen. (*Reproachfully.*) Mamma!

Lady Bracknell. In the carriage, Gwendolen! (GWEN-DOLEN *goes to the door. She and* JACK *blow kisses to each other behind* LADY BRACKNELL'*s back.* LADY BRACKNELL *looks vaguely about as if she could not understand what the noise was. Finally turns round.*) Gwendolen, the carriage!

Gwendolen. Yes, mamma. (*Goes out, looking back at* JACK.)

Lady Bracknell. (*Sitting down.*) You can take a seat, Mr. Worthing.

(*Looks in her pocket for note-book and pencil.*)

Jack. Thank you, Lady Bracknell, I prefer standing.

Lady Bracknell. (*Pencil and note-book in hand.*) I feel bound to tell you that you are not down on my list of eligible young men, although I have the same list as the dear Duchess of Bolton has. We work together, in fact. However, I am quite ready to enter your name, should your answers be what a really affectionate mother requires. Do you smoke?

Jack. Well, yes, I must admit I smoke.

Lady Bracknell. I am glad to hear it. A man should always have an occupation of some kind. There are far too many idle men in London as it is. How old are you?

Jack. Twenty-nine.

Lady Bracknell. A very good age to be married at. I have always been of opinion that a man who desires to get married should know either everything or nothing. Which do you know?

Jack. (*After some hesitation.*) I know nothing, Lady Bracknell.

Lady Bracknell. I am pleased to hear it. I do not approve of anything that tampers with natural ignorance. Ignorance is like a delicate exotic fruit; touch it and the bloom is gone. The whole theory of modern education is radically unsound. Fortunately in England, at any rate, education produces no effect whatsoever. If it did, it would prove a serious danger to the upper classes, and probably lead to acts of violence in Grosvenor Square. What is your income?

Jack. Between seven and eight thousand a year.

Lady Bracknell. (*Makes a note in her book.*) In land, or in investments?

Jack. In investments, chiefly.

Lady Bracknell. That is satisfactory. What between the duties expected of one during one's lifetime, and the duties enacted from one after one's death, land has ceased to be either a profit or a pleasure. It gives one position, and prevents one from keeping it up. That's all that can be said about land.

Jack. I have a country house with some land, of course,

attached to it, about fifteen hundred acres, I believe; but I don't depend on that for my real income. In fact, as far as I can make out, the poachers are the only people who make anything out of it.

Lady Bracknell. A country house! How many bedrooms? Well, that point can be cleared up afterwards. You have a town house, I hope? A girl with a simple, unspoiled nature, like Gwendolen, could hardly be expected to reside in the country.

Jack. Well, I own a house in Belgrave Square, but it is let by the year to Lady Bloxham. Of course, I can get it back whenever I like, at six months' notice.

Lady Bracknell. Lady Bloxham? I don't know her.

Jack. Oh, she goes about very little. She is a lady considerably advanced in years.

Lady Bracknell. Ah, nowadays that is no guarantee of respectability of character. What number in Belgrave Square?

Jack. 149.

Lady Bracknell. (*Shaking her head.*) The unfashionable side. I thought there was something. However, that could easily be altered.

Jack. Do you mean the fashion, or the side?

Lady Bracknell. (*Sternly.*) Both, if necessary, I presume. What are your politics?

Jack. Well, I am afraid I really have none. I am a Liberal Unionist.

Lady Bracknell. Oh, they count as Tories. They dine with us. Or come in the evening, at any rate. Now to minor matters. Are your parents living?

Jack. I have lost both my parents.

Lady Bracknell. To lose one parent, Mr. Worthing, may be regarded as a misfortune; to lose both seems like carelessness. Who was your father? He was evidently a man of some wealth. Was he born in what the Radical papers call the purple of commerce, or did he rise from the ranks of the aristocracy?

Jack. I am afraid I really don't know. The fact is, Lady Bracknell, I said I had lost my parents. It would be nearer the truth to say that my parents seem to have lost me. . . . I don't actually know who I am by birth. I was . . . well, I was found.

Lady Bracknell. Found!

Jack. The late Mr. Thomas Cardew, an old gentleman of a very charitable and kindly disposition, found me, and gave me the name of Worthing, because he happened to have a first-class ticket for Worthing in his pocket at the time. Worthing is a place in Sussex. It is a seaside resort.

Lady Bracknell. Where did the charitable gentleman who had a first-class ticket for this seaside resort find you?

Jack. (*Gravely.*) In a hand-bag.

Lady Bracknell. A hand-bag?

Jack. (*Very seriously.*) Yes, Lady Bracknell. I was in a hand-bag—a somewhat large, black leather hand-bag, with handles to it—an ordinary hand-bag, in fact.

Lady Bracknell. In what locality did this Mr. James, or Thomas, Cardew come across this ordinary hand-bag?

Jack. In the cloak-room at Victoria Station. It was given to him in mistake for his own.

Lady Bracknell. The cloak-room at Victoria Station?

Jack. Yes. The Brighton line.

Lady Bracknell. The line is immaterial. Mr. Worthing, I confess I feel somewhat bewildered by what you have just told me. To be born, or at any rate bred, in a hand-bag, whether it had handles or not, seems to me to display a contempt for the ordinary decencies of family life that reminds one of the worst excesses of the French Revolution. And I presume you know what that unfortunate movement led to? As for the particular locality in which the hand-bag was found, a cloak-room at a railway station might serve to conceal a social indiscretion—has probably, indeed, been used for that purpose before now—but it could hardly be regarded as an assured basis for a recognized position in good society.

Jack. May I ask you then what you would advise me to do? I need hardly say I would do anything in the world to ensure Gwendolen's happiness.

Lady Bracknell. I would strongly advise you, Mr. Worthing, to try and acquire some relations as soon as possible, and to make a definite effort to produce at any rate one parent, of either sex, before the season is quite over.

Jack. Well, I don't see how I could possibly manage to do that. I can produce the hand-bag at any moment. It is in my dressing-room at home. I really think that should satisfy you, Lady Bracknell.

Lady Bracknell. Me, sir! What has it to do with me? You can hardly imagine that I and Lord Bracknell would dream of allowing our only daughter—a girl brought up with the utmost care—to marry into a cloak-room, and form an alliance with a parcel. Good morning, Mr. Worthing!

(LADY BRACKNELL *sweeps out in majestic indignation.*)

Jack. Good morning! (ALGERNON, *from the other room, strikes up the Wedding March.* JACK *looks perfectly furious, and goes to the door.*) For goodness' sake don't play that ghastly tune, Algy! How idiotic you are!

(*The music stops and* ALGERNON *enters cheerily.*)

Algernon. Didn't it go off all right, old boy? You don't mean to say Gwendolen refused you? I know it is a way she has. She is always refusing people. I think it is most ill-natured of her.

Jack. Oh, Gwendolen is as right as a trivet. As far as she is concerned, we are engaged. Her mother is perfectly unbearable. Never met such a Gorgon. . . . I don't really know what a Gorgon is like, but I am quite sure that Lady Bracknell is one. In any case, she is a monster, without being a myth, which is rather unfair. . . . I beg your pardon, Algy, I suppose I shouldn't talk about your own aunt in that way before you.

Algernon. My dear boy, I love hearing my relations abused. It is the only thing that makes me put up with them at all. Relations are simply a tedious pack of people, who haven't got the remotest knowledge of how to live, nor the smallest instinct about when to die.

Jack. Oh, that is nonsense!

Algernon. It isn't!

Jack. Well, I won't argue about the matter. You always want to argue about things.

Algernon. That is exactly what things were originally made for.

Jack. Upon my word, if I thought that, I'd shoot myself. . . . (*A pause.*) You don't think there is any chance of Gwendolen becoming like her mother in about a hundred and fifty years, do you, Algy?

Algernon. All women become like their mothers. That is their tragedy. No man does. That's his.

Jack. Is that clever?

Algernon. It is perfectly phrased! and quite as true as any observation in civilized life should be.

Jack. I am sick to death of cleverness. Everybody is clever nowadays. You can't go anywhere without meeting clever people. The thing has become an absolute public nuisance. I wish to goodness we had a few fools left.

Algernon. We have.

Jack. I should extremely like to meet them. What do they talk about?

Algernon. The fools! Oh! about the clever people of course.

Jack. What fools!

Algernon. By the way, did you tell Gwendolen the truth about your being Ernest in town, and Jack in the country?

Jack. (*In a very patronizing manner.*) My dear fellow, the truth isn't quite the sort of thing one tells to a nice, sweet, refined girl. What extraordinary ideas you have about the way to behave to a woman!

Algernon. The only way to behave to a woman is to make love to her, if she is pretty, and to someone else, if she is plain.

Jack. Oh, that is nonsense.

Algeron. What about your brother? What about the profligate Ernest?

Jack. Oh, before the end of the week I shall have got rid of him. I'll say he died in Paris of apoplexy. Lots of people die of apoplexy, quite suddenly, don't they?

Algernon. Yes, but it's hereditary, my dear fellow. It's a sort of thing that runs in families. You had much better say a severe chill.

Jack. You are sure a severe chill isn't hereditary, or anything of that kind?

Algernon. Of course it isn't!

Jack. Very well, then. My poor brother Ernest is carried off suddenly, in Paris, by a severe chill. That gets rid of him.

Algernon. But I thought you said that . . . Miss Cardew was a little too much interested in your poor brother Ernest? Won't she feel his loss a good deal?

Jack. Oh, that is all right. Cecily is not a silly romantic girl, I am glad to say. She has got a capital appetite, goes for long walks, and pays no attention at all to her lessons.

Algernon. I would rather like to see Cecily.

Jack. I will take very good care you never do. She is excessively pretty, and she is only just eighteen.

Algernon. Have you told Gwendolen yet that you have an excessively pretty ward who is only just eighteen?

Jack. Oh! one doesn't blurt these things out to people. Cecily and Gwendolen are perfectly certain to be extremely great friends. I'll bet you anything you like that half an hour after they have met, they will be calling each other sister.

Algernon. Women only do that when they have called each other a lot of other things first. Now, my dear boy, if we want to get a good table at Willis's, we really must go and dress. Do you know it is nearly seven?

Jack. (*Irritably.*) Oh! it always is nearly seven.

Algernon. Well, I'm hungry.

Jack. I never knew you when you weren't. . . .

Algernon. What shall we do after dinner? Go to a theatre?

Jack. Oh, no! I loathe listening.

Algernon. Well, let us go to the Club?

Jack. Oh, no! I hate talking.

Algernon. Well, we might trot round to the Empire at ten?

Jack. Oh, no! I can't bear looking at things. It is so silly.

Algernon. Well, what shall we do?

Jack. Nothing!

Algernon. It is awfully hard work doing nothing. However, I don't mind hard work where there is no definite object of any kind.

(Enter LANE.*)*

Lane. Miss Fairfax.

(Enter GWENDOLEN. LANE *goes out.)*

Algernon. Gwendolen, upon my word!

Gwendolen. Algy, kindly turn your back. I have something very particular to say to Mr. Worthing.

Algernon. Really, Gwendolen, I don't think I can allow this at all.

Gwendolen. Algy, you always adopt a strictly immoral attitude towards life. You are not quite old enough to do that. (ALGERNON *retires to the fireplace.*)

Jack. My own darling!

Gwendolen. Ernest, we may never be married. From the expression on mamma's face I fear we never shall. Few parents nowadays pay any regard to what their children say to them. The old-fashioned respect for the young is fast dying out. Whatever influence I ever had over mamma, I lost at the age of three. But although she may prevent us from becoming man and wife, and I may marry someone else, and marry often, nothing that she can possibly do can alter my eternal devotion to you.

Jack. Dear Gwendolen!

Gwendolen. The story of your romantic origin, as related to me by mamma, with unpleasing comments, has naturally stirred the deeper fibres of my nature.

Your Christian name has an irresistible fascination.
The simplicity of your character makes you exquisitely
incomprehensible to me. Your town address at the
Albany I have. What is your address in the country?

Jack. The Manor House, Woolton, Hertfordshire.

(ALGERNON, *who has been carefully listening, smiles to himself, and writes the address on his shirt-cuff. Then picks up
the Railway Guide.*)

Gwendolen. There is a good postal service, I suppose?
It may be necessary to do something desperate. That of
course will require serious consideration. I will com-
municate with you daily.

Jack. My own one!

Gwendolen. How long do you remain in town?

Jack. Till Monday.

Gwendolen. Good! Algy, you may turn round now.

Algernon. Thanks, I've turned round already.

Gwendolen. You may also ring the bell.

Jack. You will let me see you to your carriage, my own
darling?

Gwendolen. Certainly.

Jack. (*To* LANE, *who now enters.*) I will see Miss Fairfax
out.

Lane. Yes, sir. (JACK *and* GWENDOLEN *go off.*)

(LANE *presents several letters on a salver, to* ALGERNON. *It is
to be surmised that they are bills, as* ALGERNON, *after looking at the envelopes, tears them up.*)

Algernon. A glass of sherry, Lane.

Lane. Yes, sir.

Algernon. Tomorrow, Lane, I'm going Bunburying.

Lane. Yes, sir.

Algernon. I shall probably not be back till Monday. You can put up my dress clothes, my smoking jacket, and all the Bunbury suits. . . .

Lane. Yes, sir. (*Handing sherry.*)

Algernon. I hope tomorrow will be a fine day, Lane.

Lane. It never is, sir.

Algernon. Lane, you're a perfect pessimist.

Lane. I do my best to give satisfaction, sir.

(*Enter* JACK. LANE *goes off.*)

Jack. There's a sensible, intellectual girl! the only girl I ever cared for in my life. (ALGERNON *is laughing immoderately.*) What on earth are you so amused at?

Algernon. Oh, I'm a little anxious about poor Bunbury, that is all.

Jack. If you don't take care, your friend Bunbury will get you into a serious scrape some day.

Algernon. I love scrapes. They are the only things that are never serious.

Jack. Oh, that's nonsense, Algy. You never talk anything but nonsense.

Algernon. Nobody ever does.

(JACK *looks indignantly at him, and leaves the room.* ALGERNON *lights a cigarette, reads his shirt-cuff, and smiles.*)

Act Drop

ACT TWO

Scene: Garden at the Manor House, Woolton. A flight of grey stone steps leads up to the house. The garden, an old-fashioned one, full of roses. Time of year, July. Basket chairs, and a table covered with books, are set under a large yew-tree.

(MISS PRISM *discovered seated at the table.* CECILY *is at the back, watering flowers.*)

Miss Prism. (*Calling.*) Cecily, Cecily! Surely such a utilitarian occupation as the watering of flowers is rather Moulton's duty than yours? Especially at a moment when intellectual pleasures await you. Your German grammar is on the table. Pray open it at page fifteen. We will repeat yesterday's lesson.

Cecily. (*Coming over very slowly.*) But I don't like German. It isn't at all a becoming language. I know perfectly well that I look quite plain after my German lesson.

Miss Prism. Child, you know how anxious your guardian is that you should improve yourself in every way. He laid particular stress on your German, as he was leaving for town yesterday. Indeed, he always lays stress on your German when he is leaving for town.

32

Cecily. Dear Uncle Jack is so very serious! Sometimes he is so serious that I think he cannot be quite well.

Miss Prism. (*Drawing herself up.*) Your guardian enjoys the best of health, and his gravity of demeanor is especially to be commended in one so comparatively young as he is. I know no one who has a higher sense of duty and responsibility.

Cecily. I suppose that is why he often looks a little bored when we three are together.

Miss Prism. Cecily! I am surprised at you. Mr. Worthing has many troubles in his life. Idle merriment and triviality would be out of place in his conversation. You must remember his constant anxiety about that unfortunate young man his brother.

Cecily. I wish Uncle Jack would allow that unfortunate young man, his brother, to come down here sometimes. We might have a good influence over him, Miss Prism. I am sure you certainly would. You know German, and geology, and things of that kind influence a man very much. (CECILY *begins to write in her diary.*)

Miss Prism. (*Shaking her head.*) I do not think that even I could produce any effect on a character that according to his own brother's admission is irretrievably weak and vacillating. Indeed I am not sure that I would desire to reclaim him. I am not in favor of this modern mania for turning bad people into good people at a moment's notice. As a man sows so let him reap. You must put away your diary, Cecily. I really don't see why you should keep a diary at all.

Cecily. I keep a diary in order to enter the wonderful secrets of my life. If I didn't write them down I should probably forget all about them.

Miss Prism. Memory, my dear Cecily, is the diary that we all carry about with us.

Cecily. Yes, but it usually chronicles the things that have never happened, and couldn't possibly have happened. I believe that Memory is responsible for nearly all the three-volume novels that Mudie sends us.

Miss Prism. Do not speak slightingly of the three-volume novel, Cecily. I wrote one myself in earlier days.

Cecily. Did you really, Miss Prism? How wonderfully clever you are! I hope it did not end happily? I don't like novels that end happily. They depress me so much.

Miss Prism. The good ended happily, and the bad unhappily. That is what Fiction means.

Cecily. I suppose so. But it seems very unfair. And was your novel ever published?

Miss Prism. Alas! no. The manuscript unfortunately was abandoned. (CECILY *starts.*) I used the word in the sense of lost or mislaid. To your work, child, these speculations are profitless.

Cecily. (*Smiling.*) But I see dear Dr. Chasuble coming up through the garden.

Miss Prism. (*Rising and advancing.*) Dr. Chasuble! This is indeed a pleasure.

(*Enter* CANON CHASUBLE.)

Chasuble. And how are we this morning? Miss Prism, you are, I trust, well?

Cecily. Miss Prism has just been complaining of a slight headache. I think it would do her so much good to have a short stroll with you in the Park, Dr. Chasuble.

Miss Prism. Cecily, I have not mentioned anything about a headache.

Cecily. No, dear Miss Prism, I know that, but I felt instinctively that you had a headache. Indeed I was thinking about that, and not about my German lesson, when the Rector came in.

Chasuble. I hope, Cecily, you are not inattentive.

Cecily. Oh, I am afraid I am.

Chasuble. That is strange. Were I fortunate enough to be Miss Prism's pupil, I would hang upon her lips. (MISS PRISM *glares*.) I spoke metaphorically.—My metaphor was drawn from bees. Ahem! Mr. Worthing, I suppose, has not returned from town yet?

Miss Prism. We do not expect him till Monday afternoon.

Chasuble. Ah yes, he usually likes to spend his Sunday in London. He is not one of those whose sole aim is enjoyment, as, by all accounts, that unfortunate young man his brother seems to be. But I must not disturb Egeria and her pupil any longer.

Miss Prism. Egeria? My name is Laetitia, Doctor.

Chasuble. (*Bowing.*) A classical allusion merely, drawn from the Pagan authors. I shall see you both no doubt at Evensong?

Miss Prism. I think, dear Doctor, I will have a stroll with you. I find I have a headache after all, and a walk might do it good.

Chasuble. With pleasure, Miss Prism, with pleasure. We might go as far as the schools and back.

Miss Prism. That would be delightful. Cecily, you will read your Political Economy in my absence. The chapter on the Fall of the Rupee you may omit. It is somewhat too sensational. Even these metallic problems have their melodramatic side.

(Goes down the garden with DR. CHASUBLE.*)*

Cecily. *(Picks up books and throws them back on table.)* Horrid Political Economy! Horrid Geography! Horrid, horrid German!

(Enter MERRIMAN *with a card on a salver.)*

Merriman. Mr. Ernest Worthing has just driven over from the station. He has brought his luggage with him.

Cecily. *(Takes the card and reads it.)* "Mr. Ernest Worthing, B.4, The Albany, W." Uncle Jack's brother! Did you tell him Mr. Worthing was in town?

Merriman. Yes, Miss. He seemed very much disappointed. I mentioned that you and Miss Prism were in the garden. He said he was anxious to speak to you privately for a moment.

Cecily. Ask Mr. Ernest Worthing to come here. I suppose you had better talk to the housekeeper about a room for him.

Merriman. Yes, Miss. (MERRIMAN *goes off.*)

Cecily. I have never met any really wicked person before. I feel rather frightened. I am so afraid he will look just like everyone else.

(Enter ALGERNON, *very gay and debonair.)*

He does!

Algernon. (*Raising his hat.*) You are my little cousin Cecily, I'm sure.

Cecily. You are under some strange mistake. I am not little. In fact, I believe I am more than usually tall for my age. (ALGERNON *is rather taken aback.*) But I am your cousin Cecily. You, I see from your card, are Uncle Jack's brother, my cousin Ernest, my wicked cousin Ernest.

Algernon. Oh! I am not really wicked at all, Cousin Cecily. You mustn't think that I am wicked.

Cecily. If you are not, then you have certainly been deceiving us all in a very inexcusable manner. I hope you have not been leading a double life, pretending to be wicked and being really good all the time. That would be hypocrisy.

Algernon. (*Looks at her in amazement.*) Oh! Of course I have been rather reckless.

Cecily. I am glad to hear it.

Algernon. In fact, now you mention the subject, I have been very bad in my own small way.

Cecily. I don't think you should be so proud of that, though I am sure it must have been very pleasant.

Algernon. It is much pleasanter being here with you.

Cecily. I can't understand how you are here at all. Uncle Jack won't be back till Monday afternoon.

Algernon. That is a great disappointment. I am obliged to go up by the first train on Monday morning. I have a business appointment that I am anxious . . . to miss.

Cecily. Couldn't you miss it anywhere but in London?

Algernon. No, the appointment is in London.

Cecily. Well, I know, of course, how important it is not to keep a business engagement, if one wants to retain any sense of the beauty of life, but still I think you had better wait till Uncle Jack arrives. I know he wants to speak to you about your emigrating.

Algernon. About my what?

Cecily. Your emigrating. He has gone up to buy your outfit.

Algernon. I certainly wouldn't let Jack buy my outfit. He has no taste in neckties at all.

Cecily. I don't think you will require neckties. Uncle Jack is sending you to Australia.

Algernon. Australia! I'd sooner die.

Cecily. Well, he said at dinner on Wednesday night, that you would have to choose between this world, the next world, and Australia.

Algernon. Oh, well! The accounts I have received of Australia and the next world are not particularly encouraging. This world is good enough for me, Cousin Cecily.

Cecily. Yes, but are you good enough for it?

Algernon. I'm afraid I'm not that. That is why I want you to reform me. You might make that your mission, if you don't mind, Cousin Cecily.

Cecily. I'm afraid I've no time, this afternoon.

Algernon. Well, would you mind my reforming myself this afternoon?

Cecily. It is rather Quixotic of you. But I think you should try.

Algernon. I will. I feel better already.

Cecily. You are looking a little worse.

Algernon. That is because I am hungry.

Cecily. How thoughtless of me. I should have remembered that when one is going to lead an entirely new life, one requires regular and wholesome meals. Won't you come in?

Algernon. Thank you. Might I have a buttonhole first? I never have any appetite unless I have a buttonhole first.

Cecily. A Maréchal Niel? (*Picks up scissors.*)

Algernon. No, I'd sooner have a pink rose.

Cecily. Why? (*Cuts a flower.*)

Algernon. Because you are like a pink rose, Cousin Cecily.

Cecily. I don't think it can be right for you to talk to me like that. Miss Prism never says such things to me.

Algernon. Then Miss Prism is a short-sighted old lady. (CECILY *puts the rose in his buttonhole.*) You are the prettiest girl I ever saw.

Cecily. Miss Prism says that all good looks are a snare.

Algernon. They are a snare that every sensible man would like to be caught in.

Cecily. Oh! I don't think I would care to catch a sensible man. I shouldn't know what to talk to him about.

(They pass into the house. MISS PRISM *and* DR. CHASUBLE *return.)*

Miss Prism. You are too much alone, dear Dr. Chasuble. You should get married. A misanthrope I can understand—a womanthrope, never!

Chasuble. *(With a scholar's shudder.)* Believe me, I do not deserve so neologistic a phrase. The precept as well as the practice of the Primitive Church was distinctly against matrimony.

Miss Prism. *(Sententiously.)* That is obviously the reason why the Primitive Church has not lasted up to the present day. And you do not seem to realize, dear Doctor, that by persistently remaining single, a man converts himself into a permanent public temptation. Men should be more careful; this very celibacy leads weaker vessels astray.

Chasuble. But is a man not equally attractive when married?

Miss Prism. No married man is ever attractive except to his wife.

Chasuble. And often, I've been told, not even to her.

Miss Prism. That depends on the intellectual sympathies of the woman. Maturity can always be depended on. Ripeness can be trusted. Young women are green. (DR. CHASUBLE *starts.*) I spoke horticulturally. My metaphor was drawn from fruits. But where is Cecily?

Chasuble. Perhaps she followed us to the schools.

(Enter JACK *slowly from the back of the garden. He is dressed in the deepest mourning, with crepe hatband and black gloves.)*

Miss Prism. Mr. Worthing!

Chasuble. Mr. Worthing?

Miss Prism. This is indeed a surprise. We did not look for you till Monday afternoon.

Jack. *(Shakes* MISS PRISM's *hand in a tragic manner.)* I have returned sooner than I expected. Dr. Chasuble, I hope you are well?

Chasuble. Dear Mr. Worthing, I trust this garb of woe does not betoken some terrible calamity?

Jack. My brother.

Miss Prism. More shameful debts and extravagance?

Chasuble. Still leading his life of pleasure?

Jack. *(Shaking his head.)* Dead!

Chasuble. Your brother Ernest dead?

Jack. Quite dead.

Miss Prism. What a lesson for him! I trust he will profit by it.

Chasuble. Mr. Worthing, I offer you my sincere condolence. You have at least the consolation of knowing that you were always the most generous and forgiving of brothers.

Jack. Poor Ernest! He had many faults, but it is a sad, sad blow.

Chasuble. Very sad indeed. Were you with him at the end?

Jack. No. He died abroad; in Paris, in fact. I had a telegram last night from the manager of the Grand Hotel.

Chasuble. Was the cause of death mentioned?

Jack. A severe chill, it seems.

Miss Prism. As a man sows, so shall he reap.

Chasuble. (*Raising his hand.*) Charity, dear Miss Prism, charity! None of us are perfect. I myself am peculiarly susceptible to draughts. Will the interment take place here?

Jack. No. He seems to have expressed a desire to be buried in Paris.

Chasuble. In Paris! (*Shakes his head.*) I fear that hardly points to any very serious state of mind at the last. You would no doubt wish me to make some slight allusion to this tragic domestic affliction next Sunday. (JACK *presses his hand convulsively.*) My sermon on the meaning of the manna in the wilderness can be adapted to almost any occasion, joyful, or, as in the present case, distressing. (*All sigh.*) I have preached it at harvest celebrations, christenings, confirmations, on days of humiliation and festal days. The last time I delivered it was in the Cathedral, as a charity sermon on behalf of the Society for the Prevention of Discontent among the Upper Orders. The Bishop, who was present, was much struck by some of the analogies I drew.

Jack. Ah! that reminds me, you mentioned christenings I think, Dr. Chasuble? I suppose you know how to christen all right? (DR. CHASUBLE *looks astounded.*) I mean, of course, you are continually christening, aren't you?

Miss Prism. It is, I regret to say, one of the Rector's most constant duties in this parish. I have often spoken to the poorer classes on the subject. But they don't seem to know what thrift is.

Chasuble. But is there any particular infant in whom you are interested, Mr. Worthing? Your brother was, I believe, unmarried, was he not?

Jack. Oh yes.

Miss Prism. (*Bitterly.*) People who live entirely for pleasure usually are.

Jack. But it is not for any child, dear Doctor. I am very fond of children. No! the fact is, I would like to be christened myself, this afternoon, if you have nothing better to do.

Chasuble. But surely, Mr. Worthing, you have been christened already?

Jack. I don't remember anything about it.

Chasuble. But have you any grave doubts on the subject?

Jack. I certainly intend to have. Of course I don't know if the thing would bother you in any way, or if you think I am a little too old now.

Chasuble. Not at all. The sprinkling, and, indeed, the immersion of adults is a perfectly canonical practice.

Jack. Immersion!

Chasuble. You need have no apprehensions. Sprinkling is all that is necessary, or indeed I think advisable. Our weather is so changeable. At what hour would you wish the ceremony performed?

Jack. Oh, I might trot round about five if that would suit you.

Chasuble. Perfectly, perfectly! In fact I have two similar ceremonies to perform at that time. A case of twins that occurred recently in one of the outlying cottages on your own estate. Poor Jenkins the carter, a most hard-working man.

Jack. Oh! I don't see much fun in being christened along with other babies. It would be childish. Would half-past five do?

Chasuble. Admirably! Admirably! (*Takes out watch.*) And now, dear Mr. Worthing, I will not intrude any longer into a house of sorrow. I would merely beg you not to be too much bowed down by grief. What seems to us bitter trials are often blessings in disguise.

Miss Prism. This seems to me a blessing of an extremely obvious kind.

(*Enter* CECILY *from the house.*)

Cecily. Uncle Jack! Oh, I am pleased to see you back. But what horrid clothes you have got on! Do go and change them.

Miss Prism. Cecily!

Chasuble. My child! my child! (CECILY *goes towards* JACK; *he kisses her brow in a melancholy manner.*)

Cecily. What is the matter, Uncle Jack? Do look happy! You look as if you had a toothache, and I have got such a surprise for you. Who do you think is in the dining-room? Your brother!

Jack. Who?

Cecily. Your brother Ernest. He arrived about half an hour ago.

Jack. What nonsense! I haven't got a brother!

Cecily. Oh, don't say that. However badly he may have behaved to you in the past he is still your brother. You couldn't be so heartless as to disown him. I'll tell him to come out. And you will shake hands with him, won't you, Uncle Jack? (*Runs back into the house.*)

Chasuble. These are very joyful tidings.

Miss Prism. After we had all been resigned to his loss, his sudden return seems to me peculiarly distressing.

Jack. My brother is in the dining-room? I don't know what it all means. I think it is perfectly absurd.

(*Enter* ALGERNON *and* CECILY *hand in hand. They come slowly up to* JACK.)

Jack. Good heavens! (*Motions* ALGERNON *away.*)

Algernon. Brother John, I have come down from town to tell you that I am very sorry for all the trouble I have given you, and that I intend to lead a better life in the future. (JACK *glares at him and does not take his hand.*)

Cecily. Uncle Jack, you are not going to refuse your own brother's hand?

Jack. Nothing will induce me to take his hand. I think his coming down here disgraceful. He knows perfectly well why.

Cecily. Uncle Jack, do be nice. There is some good in

everyone. Ernest has just been telling me about his poor invalid friend Mr. Bunbury whom he goes to visit so often. And surely there must be much good in one who is kind to an invalid, and leaves the pleasures of London to sit by a bed of pain.

Jack. Oh! he has been talking about Bunbury, has he?

Cecily. Yes, he has told me all about poor Mr. Bunbury, and his terrible state of health.

Jack. Bunbury! Well, I won't have him talk to you about Bunbury or about anything else. It is enough to drive one perfectly frantic.

Algernon. Of course I admit that the faults were all on my side. But I must say that I think that Brother John's coldness to me is peculiarly painful. I expected a more enthusiastic welcome, especially considering it is the first time I have come here.

Cecily. Uncle Jack, if you don't shake hands with Ernest, I will never forgive you.

Jack. Never forgive me?

Cecily. Never, never, never!

Jack. Well, this is the last time I shall ever do it. (*Shakes hands with* ALGERNON *and glares.*)

Chasuble. It's pleasant, is it not, to see so perfect a reconciliation? I think we might leave the two brothers together.

Miss Prism. Cecily, you will come with us.

Cecily. Certainly, Miss Prism. My little task of reconciliation is over.

Chasuble. You have done a beautiful action today, dear child.

Miss Prism. We must not be premature in our judgements.

Cecily. I feel very happy. (*They all go off except* JACK *and* ALGERNON.)

Jack. You young scoundrel, Algy, you must get out of this place as soon as possible. I don't allow any Bunburying here.

(*Enter* MERRIMAN.)

Merriman. I have put Mr. Ernest's things in the room next to yours, sir. I suppose that is all right?

Jack. What?

Merriman. Mr. Ernest's luggage, sir. I have unpacked it and put it in the room next to your own.

Jack. His luggage?

Merriman. Yes, sir. Three portmanteaus, a dressingcase, two hatboxes, and a large luncheon-basket.

Algernon. I am afraid I can't stay more than a week this time.

Jack. Merriman, order the dog-cart at once. Mr. Ernest has been suddenly called back to town.

Merriman. Yes, sir. (*Goes back into the house.*)

Algernon. What a fearful liar you are, Jack. I have not been called back to town at all.

Jack. Yes, you have.

Algernon. I haven't heard anyone call me.

Jack. Your duty as a gentleman calls you back.

Algernon. My duty as a gentleman has never interfered with my pleasures in the smallest degree.

Jack. I can quite understand that.

Algernon. Well, Cecily is a darling.

Jack. You are not to talk of Miss Cardew like that. I don't like it.

Algernon. Well, I don't like your clothes. You look perfectly ridiculous in them. Why on earth don't you go up and change? It is perfectly childish to be in deep mourning for a man who is actually staying for a whole week with you in your house as a guest. I call it grotesque.

Jack. You are certainly not staying with me for a whole week as a guest or anything else. You have got to leave . . . by the four-five train.

Algernon. I certainly won't leave you so long as you are in mourning. It would be most unfriendly. If I were in mourning you would stay with me, I suppose. I should think it very unkind if you didn't.

Jack. Well, will you go if I change my clothes?

Algernon. Yes, if you are not too long. I never saw anybody take so long to dress, and with such little result.

Jack. Well, at any rate, that is better than being always over-dressed as you are.

Algernon. If I am occasionally a little over-dressed, I make up for it by being always immensely over-educated.

Jack. Your vanity is ridiculous, your conduct an outrage, and your presence in my garden utterly absurd. However, you have got to catch the four-five, and I hope you will have a pleasant journey back to town. This Bunburying, as you call it, has not been a great success for you.

(Goes into the house.)

Algernon. I think it has been a great success. I'm in love with Cecily, and that is everything.

(Enter CECILY at the back of the garden. She picks up the can and begins to water the flowers.)

But I must see her before I go, and make arrangements for another Bunbury. Ah, there she is.

Cecily. Oh, I merely came back to water the roses. I thought you were with Uncle Jack.

Algernon. He's gone to order the dog-cart for me.

Cecily. Oh, is he going to take you for a nice drive?

Algernon. He's going to send me away.

Cecily. Then have we got to part?

Algernon. I am afraid so. It's a very painful parting.

Cecily. It is always painful to part from people whom one has known for a very brief space of time. The absence of old friends one can endure with equanimity. But even a momentary separation from anyone to whom one has just been introduced is almost unbearable.

Algernon. Thank you.

(Enter MERRIMAN.)

Merriman. The dog-cart is at the door, sir.

(ALGERNON looks appealingly at CECILY.)

Cecily. It can wait, Merriman . . . for . . . five minutes.

Merriman. Yes, Miss.

(Exit MERRIMAN.)

Algernon. I hope, Cecily, I shall not offend you if I state quite frankly and openly that you seem to me to be in every way the visible personification of absolute perfection.

Cecily. I think your frankness does you great credit, Ernest. If you will allow me, I will copy your remarks into my diary. (*Goes over to table and begins writing in diary.*)

Algernon. Do you really keep a diary? I'd give anything to look at it. May I?

Cecily. Oh no. (*Puts her hand over it.*) You see, it is simply a very young girl's record of her own thoughts and impressions, and consequently meant for publication. When it appears in volume form I hope you will order a copy. But pray, Ernest, don't stop. I delight in taking down from dictation. I have reached "absolute perfection." You can go on. I am quite ready for more.

Algernon. (*Somewhat taken aback.*) Ahem! Ahem!

Cecily. Oh, don't cough, Ernest. When one is dictating one should speak fluently and not cough. Besides, I don't know how to spell a cough. (*Writes as* ALGERNON *speaks.*)

Algernon. (*Speaking very rapidly.*) Cecily, ever since I first looked upon your wonderful and incomparable beauty, I have dared to love you wildly, passionately, devotedly, hopelessly.

Cecily. I don't think that you should tell me that you love me wildly, passionately, devotedly, hopelessly. Hopelessly doesn't seem to make much sense, does it?

Algernon. Cecily.

(Enter MERRIMAN.*)*

Merriman. The dog-car is waiting, sir.

Algernon. Tell it to come round next week, at the same hour.

Merriman. (*Looks at* CECILY, *who makes no sign.*) Yes, sir.

(MERRIMAN *retires.*)

Cecily. Uncle Jack would be very much annoyed if he knew you were staying on till next week, at the same hour.

Algernon. Oh, I don't care about Jack. I don't care for anybody in the whole world but you. I love you, Cecily. You will marry me, won't you?

Cecily. You silly boy! Of course. Why, we have been engaged for the last three months.

Algernon. For the last three months?

Cecily. Yes, it will be exactly three months on Thursday.

Algernon. But how did we become engaged?

Cecily. Well, ever since dear Uncle Jack first confessed to us that he had a younger brother who was very wicked and bad, you, of course, have formed the chief topic of conversation between myself and Miss Prism. And, of course, a man who is much talked about is always very attractive. One feels there must be something in him, after all. I daresay it was foolish of me, but I fell in love with you, Ernest.

Algernon. Darling. And when was the engagement actually settled?

Cecily. On the 14th of February last. Worn out by your entire ignorance of my existence, I determined to end the matter one way or the other, and after a long struggle with myself I accepted you under this dear old tree here. The next day I bought this little ring in your name, and this is the little bangle with the true lover's knot I promised you always to wear.

Algernon. Did I give you this? It's very pretty, isn't it?

Cecily. Yes, you've wonderfully good taste, Ernest. It's the excuse I've always given for your leading such a bad life. And this is the box in which I keep all your dear letters. (*Kneels at table, opens box, and produces letters tied up with blue ribbon.*)

Algernon. My letters! But, my own sweet Cecily, I have never written you any letters.

Cecily. You need hardly remind me of that, Ernest. I remember only too well that I was forced to write your letters for you. I wrote always three times a week, and sometimes oftener.

Algernon. Oh, do let me read them, Cecily?

Cecily. Oh, I couldn't possibly. They would make you far too conceited. (*Replaces box.*) The three you wrote me after I had broken off the engagement are so beautiful, and so badly spelled, that even now I can hardly read them without crying a little.

Algernon. But was our engagement ever broken off?

Cecily. Of course it was. On the 22nd of last March. You can see the entry if you like. (*Shows diary.*) "Today I broke off my engagement with Ernest. I feel it is better to do so. The weather still continues charming."

Algernon. But why on earth did you break it off? What had I done? I had done nothing at all. Cecily, I am very much hurt indeed to hear you broke it off. Particularly when the weather was so charming.

Cecily. It would hardly have been a really serious engagement if it hadn't been broken off at least once. But I forgave you before the week was out.

Algernon. (*Crossing to her, and kneeling.*) What a perfect angel you are, Cecily.

Cecily. You dear romantic boy. (*He kisses her, she puts her fingers through his hair.*) I hope your hair curls naturally, does it?

Algernon. Yes, darling, with a little help from others.

Cecily. I am so glad.

Algernon. You'll never break off our engagement again, Cecily?

Cecily. I don't think I could break it off now that I have actually met you. Besides, of course, there is the question of your name.

Algernon. Yes, of course. (*Nervously.*)

Cecily. You must not laugh at me, darling, but it had always been a girlish dream of mine to love someone whose name was Ernest. (ALGERNON *rises,* CECILY *also.*) There is something in that name that seems to inspire absolute confidence. I pity any poor married woman whose husband is not called Ernest.

Algernon. But, my dear child, do you mean to say you could not love me if I had some other name?

Cecily. But what name?

Algernon. Oh, any name you like—Algernon—for instance . . .

Cecily. But I don't like the name of Algernon.

Algernon. Well, my own dear, sweet, loving little darling, I really can't see why you should object to the name of Algernon. It is not at all a bad name. In fact, it is rather an aristocratic name. Half of the chaps who get into the Bankruptcy Court are called Algernon. But seriously, Cecily . . . (*Moving to her.*) if my name was Algy, couldn't you love me?

Cecily. (*Rising.*) I might respect you, Ernest, I might admire your character, but I fear that I should not be able to give you my undivided attention.

Algernon. Ahem! Cecily! (*Picking up hat.*) Your Rector here is, I suppose, thoroughly experienced in the practice of all the rites and ceremonials of the Church?

Cecily. Oh, yes. Dr. Chasuble is a most learned man. He has never written a single book, so you can imagine how much he knows.

Algernon. I must see him at once on a most important christening—I mean on most important business.

Cecily. Oh!

Algernon. I shan't be away more than half an hour.

Cecily. Considering that we have been engaged since February 14th, and that I only met you today for the first time, I think it is rather hard that you should leave me for so long a period as half an hour. Couldn't you make it twenty minutes?

Algernon. I'll be back in no time. (*Kisses her and rushes down the garden.*)

Cecily. What an impetuous boy he is! I like his hair so much. I must enter his proposal in my diary.

(Enter MERRIMAN.*)*

Merriman. A Miss Fairfax has just called to see Mr. Worthing. On very important business, Miss Fairfax states.

Cecily. Isn't Mr. Worthing in his library?

Merriman. Mr. Worthing went over in the direction of the Rectory some time ago.

Cecily. Pray ask the lady to come out here; Mr. Worthing is sure to be back soon. And you can bring tea.

Merriman. Yes, Miss.

(Goes out.)

Cecily. Miss Fairfax! I suppose one of the many good elderly women who are associated with Uncle Jack in some of his philanthropic work in London. I don't quite like women who are interested in philanthropic work. I think it is so forward of them.

(Enter MERRIMAN.*)*

Merriman. Miss Fairfax.

(Enter GWENDOLEN. *Exit* MERRIMAN.*)*

Cecily. (*Advancing to meet her.*) Pray let me introduce myself to you. My name is Cecily Cardew.

Gwendolen. Cecily Cardew? (*Moving to her and shaking hands.*) What a very sweet name! Something tells me that we are going to be great friends. I like you already more than I can say. My first impressions of people are never wrong.

Cecily. How nice of you to like me so much after we have known each other such a comparatively short time. Pray sit down.

Gwendolen. (*Still standing up.*) I may call you Cecily, may I not?

Cecily. With pleasure!

Gwendolen. And you will always call me Gwendolen, won't you?

Cecily. If you wish.

Gwendolen. Then that is all quite settled, is it not?

Cecily. I hope so. (*A pause. They both sit down together.*)

Gwendolen. Perhaps this might be a favorable opportunity for my mentioning who I am. My father is Lord Bracknell. You have never heard of papa, I suppose?

Cecily. I don't think so.

Gwendolen. Outside the family circle, papa, I am glad to say, is entirely unknown. I think that is quite as it should be. The home seems to me to be the proper sphere for the man. And certainly once a man begins to neglect his domestic duties he becomes painfully effeminate, does he not? And I don't like that. It makes men so very attractive. Cecily, mamma, whose views on education are remarkably strict, has brought me up to be extremely short-sighted; it is part of her system; so do you mind my looking at you through my glasses?

Cecily. Oh! not at all, Gwendolen. I am very fond of being looked at.

Gwendolen. (*After examining* CECILY *carefully through a lorgnette.*) You are here on a short visit, I suppose.

Cecily. Oh no! I live here.

Gwendolen. (*Severely.*) Really? Your mother, no doubt, or some female relative of advanced years, resides here also?

Cecily. Oh no! I have no mother, nor, in fact, any relations.

Gwendolen. Indeed?

Cecily. My dear guardian, with the assistance of Miss Prism, has the arduous task of looking after me.

Gwendolen. Your guardian?

Cecily. Yes, I am Mr. Worthing's ward.

Gwendolen. Oh! It is strange he never mentioned to me that he had a ward. How secretive of him! He grows more interesting hourly. I am not sure, however, that the news inspires me with feelings of unmixed delight. (*Rising and going to her.*) I am very fond of you, Cecily; I have liked you ever since I met you! But I am bound to state that now that I know that you are Mr. Worthing's ward, I cannot help expressing a wish you were—well, just a little older than you seem to be—and not quite so very alluring in appearance. In fact, if I may speak candidly—

Cecily. Pray do! I think that whenever one has anything unpleasant to say, one should always be quite candid.

Gwendolen. Well, to speak with perfect candor, Cecily, I wish that you were fully forty-two, and more than usually plain for your age. Ernest has a strong upright nature. He is the very soul of truth and honor. Disloyalty would be as impossible to him as deception. But even men of the noblest possible moral character are extremely susceptible to the influence of the physical charms of others. Modern, no less than Ancient History, supplies us with many most painful examples of what I refer to. If it were not so, indeed, History would be quite unreadable.

Cecily. I beg your pardon, Gwendolen, did you say Ernest?

Gwendolen. Yes.

Cecily. Oh, but it is not Mr. Ernest Worthing who is my guardian. It is his brother—his elder brother.

Gwendolen. (*Sitting down again.*) Ernest never mentioned to me that he had a brother.

Cecily. I am sorry to say they have not been on good terms for a long time.

Gwendolen. Ah! that accounts for it. And now that I think of it I have never heard any man mention his brother. The subject seems distasteful to most men. Cecily, you have lifted a load from my mind. I was growing almost anxious. It would have been terrible if any cloud had come across a friendship like ours, would it not? Of course you are quite, quite sure that it is not Mr. Ernest Worthing who is your guardian?

Cecily. Quite sure. (*A pause.*) In fact, I am going to be his.

Gwendolen. (*Inquiringly.*) I beg your pardon?

Cecily. (*Rather shy and confidingly.*) Dearest Gwendolen, there is no reason why I should make a secret of it to you. Our little county newspaper is sure to chronicle the fact next week. Mr. Ernest Worthing and I are engaged to be married.

Gwendolen. (*Quite politely, rising.*) My darling Cecily, I think there must be some slight error. Mr. Ernest Worthing is engaged to me. The announcement will appear in the *Morning Post* on Saturday at the latest.

Cecily. (*Very politely, rising.*) I am afraid you must be under some misconception. Ernest proposed to me exactly ten minutes ago. (*Shows diary.*)

Gwendolen. (*Examines diary through her lorgnette carefully.*) It is certainly very curious, for he asked me to be his wife yesterday afternoon at 5:30. If you would care to verify the incident, pray do so. (*Produces diary of her own.*) I never travel without my diary. One should always have something sensational to read in the train. I am so sorry, dear Cecily, if it is any disappointment to you, but I am afraid I have the prior claim.

Cecily. It would distress me more than I can tell you, dear Gwendolen, if it caused you any mental or physical anguish, but I feel bound to point out that since Ernest proposed to you he clearly has changed his mind.

Gwendolen. (*Meditatively.*) If the poor fellow has been entrapped into any foolish promise, I shall consider it my duty to rescue him at once, and with a firm hand.

Cecily. (*Thoughtfully and sadly.*) Whatever unfortunate entanglement my dear boy may have got into, I will never reproach him with it after we are married.

Gwendolen. Do you allude to me, Miss Cardew, as an entanglement? You are presumptuous. On an occasion of this kind it becomes more than a moral duty to speak one's mind. It becomes a pleasure.

Cecily. Do you suggest, Miss Fairfax, that I entrapped Ernest into an engagement? How dare you? This is no time for wearing the shallow mask of manners. When I see a spade I call it a spade.

Gwendolen. (*Satirically.*) I am glad to say that I have never seen a spade. It is obvious that our social spheres have been widely different.

(*Enter* MERRIMAN, *followed by the footman. He carries a salver, table cloth, and plate stand.* CECILY *is about to retort. The presence of the servants exercises a restraining influence, under which both girls chafe.*)

Merriman. Shall I lay tea here as usual, Miss?

Cecily. (*Sternly, in a calm voice.*) Yes, as usual. (MERRIMAN *begins to clear table and lay cloth. A long pause.* CECILY *and* GWENDOLEN *glare at each other.*)

Gwendolen. Are there many interesting walks in the vicinity, Miss Cardew?

Cecily. Oh! yes! a great many. From the top of one of the hills quite close one can see five counties.

Gwendolen. Five counties! I don't think I should like that; I hate crowds.

Cecily. (*Sweetly.*) I suppose that is why you live in

town? (GWENDOLEN *bites her lip, and beats her foot nervously with her parasol.*)

Gwendolen. (*Looking around.*) Quite a well-kept garden this is, Miss Cardew.

Cecily. So glad you like it, Miss Fairfax.

Gwendolen. I had no idea there were any flowers in the country.

Cecily. Oh, flowers are as common here, Miss Fairfax, as people are in London.

Gwendolen. Personally I cannot understand how anybody manages to exist in the country, if anybody who is anybody does. The country always bores me to death.

Cecily. Ah! This is what the newspapers call agricultural depression, is it not? I believe the aristocracy are suffering very much from it just at present. It is almost an epidemic amongst them, I have been told. May I offer you some tea, Miss Fairfax?

Gwendolen. (*With elaborate politeness.*) Thank you. (*Aside.*) Detestable girl! But I require tea!

Cecily. (*Sweetly.*) Sugar?

Gwendolen. (*Superciliously.*) No, thank you. Sugar is not fashionable any more. (CECILY *looks angrily at her, takes up the tongs and puts four lumps of sugar into the cup.*)

Cecily. (*Severely.*) Cake or bread and butter?

Gwendolen. (*In a bored manner.*) Bread and butter, please. Cake is rarely seen at the best houses nowadays.

Cecily. (*Cuts a very large slice of cake, and puts it on the tray.*) Hand that to Miss Fairfax.

(MERRIMAN *does so, and goes out with footman.*
GWENDOLEN *drinks the tea and makes a grimace. Puts down*
cup at once, reaches out her hand to the bread and butter,
looks at it, and finds it is cake.
Rises in indignation.)

Gwendolen. You have filled my tea with lumps of
sugar, and though I asked most distinctly for bread and
butter, you have given me cake. I am known for the
gentleness of my disposition, and the extraordinary
sweetness of my nature, but I warn you, Miss Cardew,
you may go too far.

Cecily. (*Rising.*) To save my poor, innocent, trusting boy
from the machinations of any other girl there are no
lengths to which I would not go.

Gwendolen. From the moment I saw you I distrusted
you. I felt that you were false and deceitful. I am never
deceived in such matters. My first impressions of people are invariably right.

Cecily. It seems to me, Miss Fairfax, that I am trespass-
ing on your valuable time. No doubt you have many
other calls of a similar character to make in the neighborhood.

(Enter JACK.*)*

Gwendolen. (*Catching sight of him.*) Ernest! My own
Ernest!

Jack. Gwendolen! Darling! (*Offers to kiss her.*)

Gwendolen. (*Drawing back.*) A moment! May I ask if
you are engaged to be married to this young lady?
(*Points to* CECILY.*)*

Jack. (*Laughing.*) To dear little Cecily! Of course not! What could have put such an idea into your pretty little head?

Gwendolen. Thank you. You may! (*Offers her cheek.*)

Cecily. (*Very sweetly.*) I knew there must be some misunderstanding, Miss Fairfax. The gentleman whose arm is at present round your waist is my dear guardian, Mr. John Worthing.

Gwendolen. I beg your pardon?

Cecily. This is Uncle Jack.

Gwendolen. (*Receding.*) Jack! Oh!

(*Enter* ALGERNON.)

Cecily. Here is Ernest.

Algernon. (*Goes straight over to* CECILY *without noticing anyone else.*) My own love! (*Offers to kiss her.*)

Cecily. (*Drawing back.*) A moment, Ernest! May I ask you—are you engaged to be married to this young lady?

Algernon. (*Looking round.*) To what young lady? Good heavens! Gwendolen!

Cecily. Yes: to good heavens, Gwendolen, I mean to Gwendolen.

Algernon. (*Laughing.*) Of course not! What could have put such an idea into your pretty little head?

Cecily. Thank you. (*Presenting her cheek to be kissed.*) You may. (ALGERNON *kisses her.*)

Gwendolen. I felt there was some slight error, Miss Cardew. The gentleman who is now embracing you is my cousin, Mr. Algernon Moncrieff.

Cecily. (*Breaking away from* ALGERNON.) Algernon Moncrieff! Oh! (*The two girls move towards each other and put their arms round each other's waists as if for protection.*)

Cecily. Are you called Algernon?

Algernon. I cannot deny it.

Cecily. Oh!

Gwendolen. Is your name really John?

Jack. (*Standing rather proudly.*) I could deny it if I liked. I could deny anything if I liked. But my name certainly is John. It has been John for years.

Cecily. (*To* GWENDOLEN.) A gross deception has been practiced on both of us.

Gwendolen. My poor wounded Cecily!

Cecily. My sweet wronged Gwendolen!

Gwendolen. (*Slowly and seriously.*) You will call me sister, will you not? (*They embrace.* JACK *and* ALGERNON *groan and walk up and down.*)

Cecily. (*Rather brightly.*) There is just one question I would like to be allowed to ask my guardian.

Gwendolen. An admirable idea! Mr. Worthing, there is just one question I would like to be permitted to put to you. Where is your brother Ernest? We are both engaged to be married to your brother Ernest, so it is a matter of some importance to us to know where your brother Ernest is at present.

Jack. (*Slowly and hesitatingly.*) Gwendolen—Cecily—it is very painful for me to be forced to speak the truth. It is the first time in my life that I have ever been reduced to such a painful position, and I am really quite inexperienced in doing anything of the kind. However, I will tell you quite frankly that I have no brother Ernest. I have no brother at all. I never had a brother in my life, and I certainly have not the smallest intention of ever having one in the future.

Cecily. (*Surprised.*) No brother at all?

Jack. (*Cheerily.*) None!

Gwendolen. (*Severely.*) Had you never a brother of any kind?

Jack. (*Pleasantly.*) Never. Not even of any kind.

Gwendolen. I am afraid it is quite clear, Cecily, that neither of us is engaged to be married to anyone.

Cecily. It is not a very pleasant position for a young girl suddenly to find herself in. Is it?

Gwendolen. Let us go into the house. They will hardly venture to come after us there.

Cecily. No, men are so cowardly, aren't they?

(*They retire into the house with scornful looks.*)

Jack. This ghastly state of things is what you call Bunburying I suppose?

Algernon. Yes, and a perfectly wonderful Bunbury it is. The most wonderful Bunbury I have ever had in my life.

Jack. Well, you've no right whatsoever to Bunbury here.

Algernon. That is absurd. One has a right to Bunbury anywhere one chooses. Every serious Bunburyist knows that.

Jack. Serious Bunburyist! Good heavens!

Algernon. Well, one must be serious about something, if one wants to have any amusement in life. I happen to be serious about Bunburying. What on earth you are serious about I haven't got the remotest idea. About everything, I should fancy. You have such an absolutely trivial nature.

Jack. Well, the only small satisfaction I have in the whole of this wretched business is that your friend Bunbury is quite exploded. You won't be able to run down to the country quite so often as you used to do, dear Algy. And a very good thing too.

Algernon. Your brother is a little off color, isn't he, dear Jack? You won't be able to disappear to London quite so frequently as your wicked custom was. And not a bad thing either.

Jack. As for your conduct towards Miss Cardew, I must say that your taking in a sweet, simple, innocent girl like that is quite inexcusable. To say nothing of the fact that she is my ward.

Algernon. I can see no possible defense at all for your deceiving a brilliant, clever, thoroughly experienced young lady like Miss Fairfax. To say nothing of the fact that she is my cousin.

Jack. I wanted to be engaged to Gwendolen, that is all, I love her.

Algernon. Well, I simply wanted to be engaged to Cecily. I adore her.

Jack. There is certainly no chance of your marrying Miss Cardew.

Algernon. I don't think there is much likelihood, Jack, of you and Miss Fairfax being united.

Jack. Well, that is no business of yours.

Algernon. If it was my business, I wouldn't talk about it. (*Begins to eat muffins.*) It is very vulgar to talk about one's business. Only people like stockbrokers do that, and then merely at dinner parties.

Jack. How you can sit there, calmly eating muffins when we are in this horrible trouble, I can't make out. You seem to me to be perfectly heartless.

Algernon. Well, I can't eat muffins in an agitated manner. The butter would probably get on my cuffs. One should always eat muffins quite calmly. It is the only way to eat them.

Jack. I say it's perfectly heartless your eating muffins at all, under the circumstances.

Algernon. When I am in trouble, eating is the only thing that consoles me. Indeed, when I am in really great trouble, as anyone who knows me intimately will tell you, I refuse everything except food and drink. At the present moment I am eating muffins because I am unhappy. Besides, I am particularly fond of muffins. (*Rising.*)

Jack. (*Rising.*) Well, that is no reason why you should eat them all in that greedy way. (*Takes muffins from* ALGERNON.)

Algernon. (*Offering tea-cake.*) I wish you would have tea-cake instead. I don't like tea-cake.

Jack. Good heavens! I suppose a man may eat his own muffins in his own garden.

Algernon. But you have just said it was perfectly heartless to eat muffins.

Jack. I said it was perfectly heartless of you, under the circumstances. That is a very different thing.

Algernon. That may be. But the muffins are the same. (*He seizes the muffin-dish from* JACK.)

Jack. Algy, I wish to goodness you would go.

Algernon. You can't possibly ask me to go without having some dinner. It's absurd. I never go without my dinner. No one ever does, except vegetarians and people like that. Besides I have just made arrangements with Dr. Chasuble to be christened at a quarter to six under the name of Ernest.

Jack. My dear fellow, the sooner you give up that nonsense the better. I made arrangements this morning with Dr. Chasuble to be christened myself at 5:30, and I naturally will take the name of Ernest. Gwendolen would wish it. We can't both be christened Ernest. It's absurd. Besides, I have a perfect right to be christened if I like. There is no evidence at all that I ever have been christened by anybody. I should think it extremely probable that I never was, and so does Dr. Chasuble. It is entirely different in your case. You have been christened already.

Algernon. Yes, but I have not been christened for years.

Jack. Yes, but you have been christened. That is the important thing.

Algernon. Quite so. So I know my constitution can

stand it. If you are not quite sure about your ever having been christened, I must say I think it rather dangerous your venturing on it now. It might make you very unwell. You can hardly have forgotten that someone very closely connected with you was very nearly carried off this week in Paris by a severe chill.

Jack. Yes, but you said yourself that a severe chill was not hereditary.

Algernon. It usen't to be, I know—but I dare say it is now. Science is always making wonderful improvements in things.

Jack. (*Picking up the muffin-dish.*) Oh, that is nonsense; you are always talking nonsense.

Algernon. Jack, you are at the muffins again! I wish you wouldn't. There are only two left. (*Takes them.*) I told you I was particularly fond of muffins.

Jack. But I hate tea-cake.

Algernon. Why on earth then do you allow tea-cake to be served up for your guests? What ideas you have of hospitality!

Jack. Algernon! I have already told you to go. I don't want you here. Why don't you go!

Algernon. I haven't quite finished my tea yet! And there is still one muffin left. (JACK *groans, and sinks into a chair.* ALGERNON *continues eating.*)

Act Drop

ACT THREE

Scene: Drawing-room at the Manor House, Woolton.
(GWENDOLEN *and* CECILY *are at the window, looking out into the garden.*)

Gwendolen. The fact that they did not follow us at once into the house, as anyone else would have done, seems to me to show that they have some sense of shame left.

Cecily. They have been eating muffins. That looks like repentance.

Gwendolen. (*After a pause.*) They don't seem to notice us at all. Couldn't you cough?

Cecily. But I haven't got a cough.

Gwendolen. They're looking at us. What effrontery!

Cecily. They're approaching. That's very forward of them.

Gwendolen. Let us preserve a dignified silence.

Cecily. Certainly. It's the only thing to do now.

(*Enter* JACK *followed by* ALGERNON. *They whistle some dreadful popular air from a British Opera.*)

Gwendolen. This dignified silence seems to produce an unpleasant effect.

Cecily. A most distasteful one.

Gwendolen. But we will not be the first to speak.

Cecily. Certainly not.

Gwendolen. Mr. Worthing, I have something very particular to ask you. Much depends on your reply.

Cecily. Gwendolen, your common sense is invaluable. Mr. Moncrieff, kindly answer me the following question. Why did you pretend to be my guardian's brother?

Algernon. In order that I might have an opportunity of meeting you.

Cecily. (*To* GWENDOLEN.) That certainly seems a satisfactory explanation, does it not?

Gwendolen. Yes, dear, if you can believe him.

Cecily. I don't. But that does not affect the wonderful beauty of his answer.

Gwendolen. True. In matters of grave importance, style, not sincerity, is the vital thing. Mr. Worthing, what explanation can you offer to me for pretending to have a brother? Was it in order that you might have an opportunity of coming up to town to see me as often as possible?

Jack. Can you doubt it, Miss Fairfax?

Gwendolen. I have the gravest doubts upon the subject. But I intend to crush them. This is not the moment for German scepticism. (*Moving to* CECILY.) Their explanations appear to be quite satisfactory, especially Mr. Worthing's. That seems to me to have the stamp of truth upon it.

Cecily. I am more than content with what Mr. Moncrieff said. His voice alone inspires one with absolute credulity.

Gwendolen. Then you think we should forgive them?

Cecily. Yes. I mean no.

Gwendolen. True! I had forgotten. There are principles at stake that one cannot surrender. Which of us should tell them? The task is not a pleasant one.

Cecily. Could we not both speak at the same time?

Gwendolen. An excellent idea! I nearly always speak at the same time as other people. Will you take the time from me?

Cecily. Certainly. (GWENDOLEN *beats time with uplifted finger.*)

Gwendolen *and* **Cecily.** (*Speaking together.*) Your Christian names are still an insuperable barrier. That is all!

Jack *and* **Algernon.** (*Speaking together.*) Our Christian names! Is that all? But we are going to be christened this afternoon.

Gwendolen. (*To* JACK.) For my sake you are prepared to do this terrible thing?

Jack. I am.

Cecily. (*To* ALGERNON.) To please me you are ready to face this fearful ordeal?

Algernon. I am!

Gwendolen. How absurd to talk of the equality of the sexes! Where questions of self-sacrifice are concerned, men are infinitely beyond us.

Jack. We are. (*Clasps hands with* ALGERNON.)

Cecily. They have moments of physical courage of which we women know absolutely nothing.

Gwendolen. (*To* JACK.) Darling!

Algernon. (*To* CECILY.) Darling. (*They fall into each other's arms.*)

(*Enter* MERRIMAN. *When he enters he coughs loudly, seeing the situation.*)

Merriman. Ahem! Ahem! Lady Bracknell.

Jack. Good heavens!

(*Enter* LADY BRACKNELL. *The couples separate in alarm. Exit* MERRIMAN.)

Lady Bracknell. Gwendolen! What does this mean?

Gwendolen. Merely that I am engaged to be married to Mr. Worthing, mamma.

Lady Bracknell. Come here. Sit down. Sit down immediately. Hesitation of any kind is a sign of mental decay in the young, of physical weakness in the old. (*Turns to* JACK.) Apprised, sir, of my daughter's sudden flight by her trusty maid, whose confidence I purchased by means of a small coin, I followed her at once by a luggage train. Her unhappy father is, I am glad to say, under the impression that she is attending a more than usually lengthy lecture by the University Extension Scheme on the Influence of a Permanent Income on Thought. I do not propose to undeceive him. Indeed I have never undeceived him on any question. I would consider it wrong. But of course, you

will clearly understand that all communication
between yourself and my daughter must cease immediately from this moment. On this point, as indeed on
all points, I am firm.

Jack. I am engaged to be married to Gwendolen, Lady
Bracknell!

Lady Bracknell. You are nothing of the kind, sir. And
now, as regards Algernon! . . . Algernon!

Algernon. Yes, Aunt Augusta.

Lady Bracknell. May I ask if it is in this house that your
invalid friend Mr. Bunbury resides?

Algernon. (*Stammering.*) Oh! No! Bunbury doesn't live
here. Bunbury is somewhere else at present. In fact,
Bunbury is dead.

Lady Bracknell. Dead! When did Mr. Bunbury die? His
death must have been extremely sudden.

Algernon. (*Airily.*) Oh! I killed Bunbury this afternoon.
I mean poor Bunbury died this afternoon.

Lady Bracknell. What did he die of?

Algernon. Bunbury? Oh, he was quite exploded.

Lady Bracknell. Exploded! Was he the victim of a rev-
olutionary outrage? I was not aware that Mr. Bunbury
was interested in social legislation. If so, he is well
punished for his morbidity.

Algernon. My dear Aunt Augusta, I mean he was
found out! The doctors found out that Bunbury could
not live, that is what I mean—so Bunbury died.

Lady Bracknell. He seems to have had great confidence
in the opinion of his physicians. I am glad, however, that

he made up his mind at the last to some definite course of action, and acted under proper medical advice. And now that we have finally got rid of this Mr. Bunbury, may I ask, Mr. Worthing, who is that young person whose hand my nephew Algernon is now holding in what seems to me a peculiarly unnecessary manner?

Jack. That lady is Miss Cecily Cardew, my ward. (LADY BRACKNELL *bows coldly to* CECILY.)

Algernon. I am engaged to be married to Cecily, Aunt Augusta.

Lady Bracknell. I beg your pardon?

Cecily. Mr. Moncrieff and I are engaged to be married, Lady Bracknell.

Lady Bracknell. (*With a shiver, crossing to the sofa and sitting down.*) I do not know whether there is anything peculiarly exciting in the air of this particular part of Hertfordshire, but the number of engagements that go on seems to me considerably above the proper average that statistics have laid down for our guidance. I think some preliminary inquiry on my part would not be out of place. Mr. Worthing, is Miss Cardew at all connected with any of the larger railway stations in London? I merely desire information. Until yesterday I had no idea that there were any families or persons whose origin was a Terminus. (JACK *looks perfectly furious, but restrains himself.*)

Jack. (*In a cold, clear voice.*) Miss Cardew is the granddaughter of the late Mr. Thomas Cardew of 149 Belgrave Square, S.W.; Gervase Park, Dorking, Surrey; and the Sporran, Fifeshire, N.B.

Lady Bracknell. That sounds not unsatisfactory. Three addresses always inspire confidence, even in trades-men. But what proof have I of their authenticity?

Jack. I have carefully preserved the Court Guides of the period. They are open to your inspection, Lady Bracknell.

Lady Bracknell. (*Grimly.*) I have known strange errors in that publication.

Jack. Miss Cardew's family solicitors are Messrs. Markby, Markby, and Markby.

Lady Bracknell. Markby, Markby, and Markby? A firm of the very highest position in their profession. Indeed I am told that one of the Mr. Markbys is occasionally to be seen at dinner parties. So far I am satisfied.

Jack. (*Very irritably.*) How extremely kind of you, Lady Bracknell! I have also in my possession, you will be pleased to hear, certificates of Miss Cardew's birth, baptism, whooping cough, registration, vaccination, confirmation, and the measles; both the German and the English variety.

Lady Bracknell. Ah! A life crowded with incident, I see; though perhaps somewhat too exciting for a young girl. I am not myself in favor of premature experiences. (*Rises, looks at her watch.*) Gwendolen! the time approaches for our departure. We have not a moment to lose. As a matter of form, Mr. Worthing, I had better ask you if Miss Cardew has any little fortune?

Jack. Oh! about a hundred and thirty thousand pounds in the Funds. That is all. Good-bye, Lady Bracknell. So pleased to have seen you.

Lady Bracknell. (*Sitting down again.*) A moment, Mr. Worthing. A hundred and thirty thousand pounds! And in the Funds! Miss Cardew seems to me a most attractive young lady, now that I look at her. Few girls of the present day have any really solid qualities, any of the qualities that last, and improve with time. We live, I regret to say, in an age of surfaces. (*To* CECILY.) Come over here, dear. (CECILY *goes across.*) Pretty child! your dress is sadly simple, and your hair seems almost as nature might have left it. But we can soon alter all that. A thoroughly experienced French maid produces a really marvelous result in a very brief space of time. I remember recommending one to young Lady Lancing, and after three months her own husband did not know her.

Jack. And after six months nobody knew her.

Lady Bracknell. (*Glares at* JACK *for a few moments. Then bends, with a practiced smile, to* CECILY.) Kindly turn round, sweet child. (CECILY *turns completely round.*) No, the side view is what I want. (CECILY *presents her profile.*) Yes, quite as I expected. There are distinct social possibilities in your profile. The two weak points in our age are its want of principle and its want of profile. The chin a little higher, dear. Style largely depends on the way the chin is worn. They are worn very high, just at present, Algernon!

Algernon. Yes, Aunt Augusta!

Lady Bracknell. There are distinct social possibilities in Miss Cardew's profile.

Algernon. Cecily is the sweetest, dearest, prettiest girl in the whole world. And I don't care twopence about social possibilities.

Lady Bracknell. Never speak disrespectfully of Society, Algernon. Only people who can't get into it do that. (*To* CECILY.) Dear child, of course you know that Algernon has nothing but his debts to depend upon. But I do not approve of mercenary marriages. When I married Lord Bracknell I had no fortune of any kind. But I never dreamed for a moment of allowing that to stand in my way. Well, I suppose I must give my consent.

Algernon. Thank you, Aunt Augusta.

Lady Bracknell. Cecily, you may kiss me!

Cecily. (*Kisses her.*) Thank you, Lady Bracknell.

Lady Bracknell. You may also address me as Aunt Augusta for the future.

Cecily. Thank you, Aunt Augusta.

Lady Bracknell. The marriage, I think, had better take place quite soon.

Algernon. Thank you, Aunt Augusta.

Cecily. Thank you, Aunt Augusta.

Lady Bracknell. To speak frankly, I am not in favor of long engagements. They give people the opportunity of finding out each other's character before marriage, which I think is never advisable.

Jack. I beg your pardon for interrupting you, Lady Bracknell, but this engagement is quite out of the question. I am Miss Cardew's guardian, and she cannot marry without my consent until she comes of age. That consent I absolutely decline to give.

Lady Bracknell. Upon what grounds, may I ask? Algernon is an extremely, I may almost say an ostentatiously, eligible young man. He has nothing, but he looks everything. What more can one desire?

Jack. It pains me very much to have to speak frankly to you, Lady Bracknell, about your nephew, but the fact is that I do not approve at all of his moral character. I suspect him of being untruthful. (ALGERNON *and* CECILY *look at him in indignant amazement.*)

Lady Bracknell. Untruthful! My nephew Algernon? Impossible! He is an Oxonian.

Jack. I fear there can be no possible doubt about the matter. This afternoon, during my temporary absence in London on an important question of romance, he obtained admission to my house by means of the false pretense of being my brother. Under an assumed name he drank, I've just been informed by my butler, an entire pint bottle of my Perrier-Jouet, Brut, '89; wine I was specially reserving for myself. Continuing his disgraceful deception, he succeeded in the course of the afternoon in alienating the affections of my only ward. He subsequently stayed to tea, and devoured every single muffin. And what makes his conduct all the more heartless is, that he was perfectly well aware from the first that I have no brother, that I never had a brother, and that I don't intend to have a brother, not even of any kind. I distinctly told him so myself yesterday afternoon.

Lady Bracknell. Ahem! Mr. Worthing, after careful consideration I have decided entirely to overlook my nephew's conduct to you

Jack. That is very generous of you, Lady Bracknell. My own decision, however, is unalterable. I decline to give my consent.

Lady Bracknell. (*To* CECILY.) Come here, sweet child. (CECILY *goes over.*) How old are you, dear?

Cecily. Well, I am really only eighteen, but I always admit to twenty when I go to evening parties.

Lady Bracknell. You are perfectly right in making some slight alteration. Indeed, no woman should ever be quite accurate about her age. It looks so calculating. . . . (*In a meditative manner.*) Eighteen, but admitting to twenty at evening parties. Well, it will not be very long before you are of age and free from the restraints of tutelage. So I don't think your guardian's consent is, after all, a matter of any importance.

Jack. Pray excuse me, Lady Bracknell, for interrupting you again, but it is only fair to tell you that according to the terms of her grandfather's will Miss Cardew does not come legally of age till she is thirty-five.

Lady Bracknell. That does not seem to me to be a grave objection. Thirty-five is a very attractive age. London society is full of women of the very highest birth who have, of their own free choice, remained thirty-five for years. Lady Dumbleton is an instance in point. To my own knowledge she has been thirty-five ever since she arrived at the age of forty, which was many years ago now. I see no reason why our dear Cecily should not be even still more attractive at the age you mention than she is at present. There will be a large accumulation of property.

Cecily. Algy, could you wait for me till I was thirty-five?

Algernon. Of course I could, Cecily. You know I could.

Cecily. Yes, I felt it instinctively, but I couldn't wait all that time. I hate waiting even five minutes for anybody. It always makes me rather cross. I am not punctual myself, I know, but I do like punctuality in others, and waiting, even to be married, is quite out of the question.

Algernon. Then what is to be done, Cecily?

Cecily. I don't know, Mr. Moncrieff.

Lady Bracknell. My dear Mr. Worthing, as Miss Cardew states positively that she cannot wait till she is thirty-five—a remark which I am bound to say seems to me to show a somewhat impatient nature—I would beg of you to reconsider your decision.

Jack. But my dear Lady Bracknell, the matter is entirely in your own hands. The moment you consent to my marriage with Gwendolen, I will most gladly allow your nephew to form an alliance with my ward.

Lady Bracknell. (*Rising and drawing herself up.*) You must be quite aware that what you propose is out of the question.

Jack. Then a passionate celibacy is all that any of us can look forward to.

Lady Bracknell. That is not the destiny I propose for Gwendolen. Algernon, of course, can choose for himself. (*Pulls out her watch.*) Come, dear (GWENDOLEN *rises.*), we have already missed five, if not six, trains. To miss any more might expose us to comment on the platform.

(Enter DR. CHASUBLE.*)*

Chasuble. Everything is quite ready for the christenings.

Lady Bracknell. The christenings, sir! Is not that somewhat premature?

Chasuble. (*Looking rather puzzled, and pointing to* JACK *and* ALGERNON.) Both these gentlemen have expressed a desire for immediate baptism.

Lady Bracknell. At their age? The idea is grotesque and irreligious! Algernon, I forbid you to be baptized. I will not hear of such excesses. Lord Bracknell would be highly displeased if he learned that that was the way in which you wasted your time and money.

Chasuble. Am I to understand then that there are to be no christenings at all this afternoon?

Jack. I don't think that, as things are now, it would be of much practical value to either of us, Dr. Chasuble.

Chasuble. I am grieved to hear such sentiments from you, Mr. Worthing. They savor of the heretical views of the Anabaptists, views that I have completely refuted in four of my unpublished sermons. However, as your present mood seems to be one peculiarly secular, I will return to the church at once. Indeed, I have just been informed by the pew-opener that for the last hour and a half Miss Prism has been waiting for me in the vestry.

Lady Bracknell. (*Starting.*) Miss Prism! Did I hear you mention a Miss Prism?

Chasuble. Yes, Lady Bracknell. I am on my way to join her.

Lady Bracknell. Pray allow me to detain you for a moment. This matter may prove to be one of vital importance to Lord Bracknell and myself. Is this Miss Prism a female of repellent aspect, remotely connected with education?

Chasuble. (*Somewhat indignantly.*) She is the most culti-vated of ladies, and the very picture of respectability.

Lady Bracknell. It is obviously the same person. May I ask what position she holds in your household?

Chasuble. (*Severely.*) I am a celibate, madam.

Jack. (*Interposing.*) Miss Prism, Lady Bracknell, has been for the last three years Miss Cardew's esteemed governess and valued companion.

Lady Bracknell. In spite of what I hear of her, I must see her at once. Let her be sent for.

Chasuble. (*Looking off.*) She approaches; she is nigh.

(*Enter* MISS PRISM *hurriedly.*)

Miss Prism. I was told you expected me in the vestry, dear Canon. I have been waiting for you there for an hour and three-quarters. (*Catches sight of* LADY BRACK-NELL, *who has fixed her with a stony glare.* MISS PRISM *grows pale and quails. She looks anxiously round as if desirous to escape.*)

Lady Bracknell. (*In a severe, judicial voice.*) Prism! (MISS PRISM *bows her head in shame.*) Come here, Prism! (MISS PRISM *approaches in a humble manner.*) Prism! Where is that baby? (*General consternation. The* CANON *starts back in horror.* ALGERNON *and* JACK *pretend to be anxious to shield* CECILY *and* GWENDOLEN *from hearing the details of a* *terrible public scandal.*) Twenty-eight years ago, Prism, you left Lord Bracknell's house, Number 104, Upper Grosvenor Street, in charge of a perambulator that contained a baby of the male sex. You never returned. A few weeks later, through the elaborate investiga- tions of the Metropolitan police, the perambulator was discovered at midnight standing by itself in a remote corner of Bayswater. It contained the manu- script of a three-volume novel of more than usually revolting sentimentality. (MISS PRISM *starts in involun- tary indignation.*) But the baby was not there. (*Everyone looks at* MISS PRISM.) Prism! Where is that baby? (*A pause.*)

Miss Prism. Lady Bracknell, I admit with shame that I do not know. I only wish I did. The plain facts of the case are these. On the morning of the day you men- tion, a day that is forever branded on my memory, I prepared as usual to take the baby out in its perambu- lator. I had also with me a somewhat old, but capacious hand-bag in which I had intended to place the manu- script of a work of fiction that I had written during my few unoccupied hours. In a moment of mental abstraction, for which I can never forgive myself, I deposited the manuscript in the bassinette, and placed the baby in the hand-bag.

Jack. (*Who has been listening attentively.*) But where did you deposit the hand-bag?

Miss Prism. Do not ask me, Mr. Worthing.

Jack. Miss Prism, this is a matter of no small impor- tance to me. I insist on knowing where you deposited the hand-bag that contained that infant.

Miss Prism. I left it in the cloak-room of one of the larger railway stations in London.

Jack. What railway station?

Miss Prism. (*Quite crushed.*) Victoria. The Brighton line. (*Sinks into a chair.*)

Jack. I must retire to my room for a moment. Gwendolen, wait here for me.

Gwendolen. If you are not too long, I will wait here for you all my life. (*Exit* JACK *in great excitement.*)

Chasuble. What do you think this means, Lady Bracknell?

Lady Bracknell. I dare not even suspect, Dr. Chasuble. I need hardly tell you that in families of high position strange coincidences are not supposed to occur. They are hardly considered the thing.

(*Noises heard overhead as if someone was throwing trunks about. Everyone looks up.*)

Cecily. Uncle Jack seems strangely agitated.

Chasuble. Your guardian has a very emotional nature.

Lady Bracknell. This noise is extremely unpleasant. It sounds as if he was having an argument. I dislike arguments of any kind. They are always vulgar, and often convincing.

Chasuble. (*Looking up.*) It has stopped now. (*The noise is redoubled.*)

Lady Bracknell. I wish he would arrive at some conclusion.

Gwendolen. This suspense is terrible. I hope it will last.

(Enter JACK *with a hand-bag of black leather in his hand.)*

Jack. (*Rushing over to* MISS PRISM.) Is this the hand-bag, Miss Prism? Examine it carefully before you speak. The happiness of more than one life depends on your answer.

Miss Prism. (*Calmly.*) It seems to be mine. Yes, here is the injury it received through the upsetting of a Gower Street omnibus in younger and happier days. Here is the stain on the lining caused by the explosion of a temperance beverage, an incident that occurred at Leamington. And here, on the lock, are my initials. I had forgotten that in an extravagant mood I had had them placed there. The bag is undoubtedly mine. I am delighted to have it so unexpectedly restored to me. It has been a great inconvenience being without it all these years.

Jack. (*In a pathetic voice.*) Miss Prism, more is restored to you than this hand-bag. I was the baby you placed in it.

Miss Prism. (*Amazed.*) You?

Jack. (*Embracing her.*) Yes . . . mother!

Miss Prism. (*Recoiling in indignant astonishment.*) Mr. Worthing, I am unmarried!

Jack. Unmarried! I do not deny that is a serious blow. But after all, who has the right to cast a stone against one who has suffered? Cannot repentance wipe out an act of folly? Why should there be one law for men, and another for women? Mother, I forgive you. (*Tries to embrace her again.*)

Miss Prism. (*Still more indignant.*) Mr. Worthing, there is some error. (*Pointing to* LADY BRACKNELL.) There is the lady who can tell you who you really are.

Jack. (*After a pause.*) Lady Bracknell, I hate to seem inquisitive, but would you kindly inform me who I am?

Lady Bracknell. I am afraid that the news I have to give you will not altogether please you. You are the son of my poor sister, Mrs. Moncrieff, and consequently Algernon's elder brother.

Jack. Algy's elder brother! Then I have a brother after all. I knew I had a brother! I always said I had a brother! Cecily,—how could you have ever doubted that I had a brother? (*Seizes hold of* ALGERNON.) Dr. Chasuble, my unfortunate brother. Miss Prism, my unfortunate brother. Gwendolen, my unfortunate brother. Algy, you young scoundrel, you will have to treat me with more respect in the future. You have never behaved to me like a brother in all your life.

Algernon. Well, not till today, old boy, I admit. I did my best, however, though I was out of practice.

(Shakes hands.)

Gwendolen. (*To* JACK.) My own! But what own are you? What is your Christian name, now that you have become someone else?

Jack. Good heavens! . . . I had quite forgotten that point. Your decision on the subject of my name is irrevocable, I suppose?

Gwendolen. I never change, except in my affections.

Cecily. What a noble nature you have, Gwendolen!

Jack. Then the question had better be cleared up at once.

Aunt Augusta, a moment. At the time when Miss Prism left me in the hand-bag, had I been christened already?

Lady Bracknell. Every luxury that money could buy, including christening, had been lavished on you by your fond and doting parents.

Jack. Then I was christened! That is settled. Now, what name was I given? Let me know the worst.

Lady Bracknell. Being the eldest son you were naturally christened after your father.

Jack. (*Irritably.*) Yes, but what was my father's Christian name?

Lady Bracknell. (*Meditatively.*) I cannot at the present moment recall what the General's Christian name was. But I have no doubt he had one. He was eccentric, I admit. But only in later years. And that was the result of the Indian climate, and marriage, and indigestion, and other things of that kind.

Jack. Algy! Can't you recollect what our father's Christian name was?

Algernon. My dear boy, we were never even on speaking terms. He died before I was a year old.

Jack. His name would appear in the Army Lists of the period, I suppose, Aunt Augusta.

Lady Bracknell. The General was essentially a man of peace, except in his domestic life. But I have no doubt his name would appear in any military directory.

Jack. The Army Lists of the last forty years are here. These delightful records should have been my constant study. (*Rushes to bookcase and tears the books out.*) M. Generals . . . Mallam, Maxbohm, Magley—what ghastly names they have—Markby, Migsby, Mobbs, Moncrieff! Lieutenant 1840, Captain, Lieutenant-Colonel, Colonel, General 1869, Christian names, Ernest John. (*Puts book very quietly down and speaks quite calmly.*) I always told you, Gwendolen, my name was Ernest, didn't I? Well, it is Ernest after all. I mean it naturally is Ernest.

Lady Bracknell. Yes, I remember now that the General was called Ernest. I knew I had some particular reason for disliking the name.

Gwendolen. Ernest! My own Ernest! I felt from the first that you could have no other name!

Jack. Gwendolen, it is a terrible thing for a man to find out suddenly that all his life he has been speaking nothing but the truth. Can you forgive me?

Gwendolen. I can. For I feel that you are sure to change.

Jack. My own one!

Chasuble. (*To* MISS PRISM.) Laetitia! (*Embraces her.*)

Miss Prism. (*Enthusiastically.*) Frederick! At last!

Algernon. Cecily! (*Embraces her.*) At last!

Jack. Gwendolen! (*Embraces her.*) At last!

Lady Bracknell. My nephew, you seem to be displaying signs of triviality.

Jack. On the contrary, Aunt Augusta, I've now realized for the first time in my life the vital Importance of Being Earnest.

Tableau

Curtain

CONNECTIONS

A subject that is beautiful in itself gives no suggestion to the artist. It lacks imperfection.

Oscar Wilde

For Anne Gregory
William Butler Yeats

"Never shall a young man,
Thrown into despair
By those great honey-coloured
Ramparts at your ear,
Love you for yourself alone
And not your yellow hair."

"But I can get a hair-dye
And set such colour there,
Brown, or black, or carrot,
That young men in despair
May love me for myself alone
And not my yellow hair."

"I heard an old religious man
But yesternight declare
That he had found a text to prove
That only God, my dear,
Could love you for yourself alone
And not your yellow hair."

■ ■ ■

Friendship is far more tragic than love. It lasts longer.

Oscar Wilde

Taking the Manly Way Out
Dave Barry

Today we're going to explore the mysterious topic of How Guys Think, which has baffled women in general, and the editors of *Cosmopolitan* magazine in particular, for thousands of years.

The big question, of course, is: How come guys never call? After successful dates, I mean. You single women out there know what I'm talking about. You go out with a guy, and you have a great time, and he seems to have a great time, and at the end of the evening he says, quote, "Can I call you?" And you, interpreting this to mean "Can I call you?", answer: "Sure!"

The instant you say this, the guy's body starts to dematerialize. Within a few seconds you can stick a tire iron right through him and wave it around; in a few more seconds he has vanished entirely, gone into the mysterious Guy Bermuda Triangle, where whole squadrons of your dates have disappeared over the years, never to be heard from again.

Eventually you start to wonder if there's something wrong with you, some kind of emotional hang-up or personality defect that your dates are detecting. Or possibly foot odor. You start having long, searching discussions with your women friends in which you say things like: "He really seemed to like me" and "I didn't feel as though I was putting pressure on him" and "Would you mind, strictly as a friend, smelling my feet?"

This is silly. There's nothing wrong with you. In fact, you should interpret the behavior of your dates as a kind of guy *compliment* to you. Because when the guy asks you if he can call you, what he's really asking you, in

Guy Code, is will you marry him. Yes. See, your basic
guy is into a straight-ahead, bottom-line kind of thought
process that does not work nearly as well with the infinitely subtle complexities of human relationships as it
does with calculating how much gravel is needed to cover
a given driveway. So here's what the guy is thinking: If he
calls you, you'll go out again, and you'll probably have
another great time, so you'll probably go out again and
have *another* great time, and so on until the only possible
option will be to get married. This is classic Guy Logic.

So when you say "Sure!" in a bright cheery voice, you
may think you're simply indicating a willingness to go out
again, but as far as he's concerned you're endorsing a lifetime commitment that he is quite frankly not ready to
make after only one date, so he naturally decided he can
never see you again. From that day forward, if he spots
you on the street, he'll spring in the opposite direction to
avoid the grave risk that the two of you might meet,
which would mean he'd have to ask you if you wanted to
get a cup of coffee, and you might say yes, and pretty
soon you'd be enjoying each other's company again, and
suddenly a clergyman would appear at your table and
YOU'D HAVE TO GET MARRIED AIEEEEEEE.

(You women think this is crazy, right? Whereas you
guys out there are nodding your heads.)

So my advice for single women is that if you're on a
date with a guy you like, and he asks whether he can call
you, you should give him a nonthreatening answer, such as:
"No."

Or: "I guess so, but bear in mind that I'm a nun."

This will make him comfortable about seeing you
again, each time gaining the courage to approach you
more closely, in the manner of a timid, easily startled
woodland creature such as a chipmunk. In a few years,

if the two of you really do have common interests and compatible personalities, you may reach the point where he'll be willing to take the Big Step, namely, eating granola directly from your hand.

No matter how close you become, however, remember this rule: Do not pressure the guy to share his most sensitive innermost thoughts and feelings with you. Guys hate this, and I'll tell you why: If you were to probe inside the guy psyche, beneath that macho exterior and the endless droning about things like the 1978 World Series, you would find, deep down inside, a passionate, heartfelt interest in: the 1978 World Series. Yes. The truth is, guys don't *have* any sensitive innermost thoughts and feelings. It's time you women knew! All these years you've been agonizing about how to make the relationship work, wondering how come he never talks to you, worrying about all the anguished emotion he must have bottled up inside, and meanwhile he's fretting about how maybe he needs longer golf spikes. I'm sorry to have to tell you this. Maybe you *should* become a nun.

Anyway, I hope I've cleared up any lingering questions anybody might have regarding guys, as a gender. For some reason I feel compelled to end this with a personal note: Heather Campbell, if you're out there, I just want to say that I had a really nice time taking you to the Junior Prom in 1964, and I was a total jerk for never, not once, mentioning this fact to you personally.

■ ■ ■

*The English are always
degrading truths into facts.
When a truth becomes
a fact it loses all its
intellectual value.*

Oscar Wilde

Oscar Wilde Goes West
Margaret Malkind

"To get on in society nowadays," Oscar Wilde said, "one has either to feed people or to shock them." In the early 1880s Wilde was just another relatively poor, prize-winning Oxford graduate who had to his credit one book of poems published at his own expense. He could not feed people, so he set out to shock them by saying the unexpected, dressing in extraordinary fashions, and espousing an exotic cause. Wilde was an apostle of aestheticism, the movement of the late nineteenth century advocating "art for art's sake."

Epigrams, polished in private, rolled off his tongue. "Nothing succeeds like excess," he said, and "Give me the luxuries and I can dispense with the necessities." Once, when he arrived very late for a luncheon party and his hostess pointed to the clock, Wilde asked, "And what, madam, do you think that little clock knows of what the great golden sun is doing?" Wilde enjoyed playing the languid dandy, hiring a cab to take him from one side of the street to the other. He once insisted that he stayed up all night with an ill primrose picked in the woods. Another time he admitted having spent the morning removing a comma from the proof of one of his poems, only to replace it in the afternoon.

To Wilde the costume of seventeenth-century cavaliers was the perfect clothing for men, and so he went about in a velvet coat, knee breeches, a loose shirt with a turndown collar, and a flowing tie. He wore his hair long. And he frequently carried a lily or a sunflower in his hand. This was an "aesthetic costume," part of his rebellion against the ugliness of Victorian dress, furniture, and machine-made articles. The aesthetes came out for Chippendales,[1] dadoes, stained glass, blue and white china, anything Japanese, and the sunflower and lily as the flowers with the most beautiful design.

Wilde's techniques for attracting public attention worked. When he overheard a man in the street grumble, "There goes that bloody fool, Oscar Wilde," he remarked delightedly to his companion, "It's extraordinary how soon one gets known in London." More publicity came to Wilde through Gilbert and Sullivan's play *Patience*. When it opened in London in 1881 and Reginald Bunthorne, "the fleshy poet," sang:

> Though the Philistines may jostle, you will rank
> as an apostle in the aesthetic band,
> If you walk down Piccadilly with a poppy or a lilly
> in your mediaeval hand,

every eye was on the unflappable Oscar sitting in the stalls.

Patience had its spin-offs: popular songs published in England and America such as the "Oscar Wilde Forget-Me-Not Waltzes," the "Oscar Polka Mazurka," "Oscar Dear," "My Aesthetic Love or Utterly, Utter, Consummate Too Too," and others. The covers of this sheet music tended to sport sunflowers, lilies, Japanese fans, blue china, and peacock feathers; the lyrics were invariably satirical.

By now Oscar Wilde the aesthete was well-known in America, and Mrs. Frank Leslie, publisher of *Frank Leslie's Illustrated Newspaper* (and later the wife of Oscar's brother Willie), suggested that Wilde give a series

---

1. Chippendales (chip'ən dālz'): Eighteenth-century English style of furniture named after Thomas Chippendale (1718–79), English cabinetmaker.

of lectures in this country. Richard D'Oyly Carte, the
Producer of Gilbert and Sullivan, immediately saw the
benefits of a lecture tour by Oscar Wilde. D'Oyly Carte's
London *Patience* had just opened. Oscar's lectures would
confound the pirates of *Patience* while publicizing the
original. But would Oscar go?

Oscar would, because he needed the money. More-
over, he had written a play, *Vera; Or, The Nihilists,* which
nobody in London would touch (nihilism hardly being
favored in monarchies after the assassination of Czar
Alexander II). Perhaps New York would find the subject
less explosive. With a contract for one-third of the box
office receipts and all expenses paid, Oscar boarded the
Arizona on Christmas Eve, 1881, ready to act out his own
aphorism that "life imitates art far more than art
imitates life." Oscar Wilde would become the theatrical
character Reginald Bunthorne[2] in the flesh.

As the flesh ran over six feet and looked more athletic
than aesthetic, the reporters who thronged aboard ship to
interview Wilde in New York were disappointed. But his
attire—a bottle green, fur-lined overcoat, round sealskin
cap set on shoulder-length hair, and yellow kid gloves—
mollified them. And his first remarks made the kind of
copy they were looking for. He told the customs agent he
had nothing to declare except his genius and called the
Atlantic a "disappointment." He later condemned Niagara
Falls too. "Every American bride," he said, "is taken there
and the sight of the stupendous waterfall must be one of the
earliest, if not the keenest, disappointments in American
married life."

Wilde was a success in New York; so D'Oyly Carte's
business manager, Colonel Morse, booked him for a

---

2. **Reginald Bunthorne:** a character from Gilbert and Sullivan's *Bunthorne,* an
operetta satirizing Wilde and his fellow aesthetes.

lecture circuit in the East and Midwest. His reception everywhere took on a familiar pattern. Hordes of reporters, usually hostile, interviewed him; businessmen used his name in their ads; the ladies, with lilies in their hair, lionized him; and the public greedily bought up tickets. People did not really come to hear what he had to say in his uninteresting monotone about "The English Renaissance," "Interior and Exterior Decoration of Houses," or "Art and the Handicraftsman." They came to see the Great Aesthete in velvet jacket and knee breeches, silk stockings and buckle shoes, Bryonic collar and tie, and long hair parted "at the equator."

His remarks on American cities and their decoration were outspoken. He dealt Chicago a mortal blow when he called its beloved water tower a "castellated monstrosity." He telegraphed back to the mayor of Griggsville, Kansas, who had asked him to lecture on aesthetics, "Begin by changing the name of your town." And he told a Baltimore audience that Washington had too many bronze generals.

Only Boston, the "Athens of America," forgot its manners and breached the rules of courtesy to a foreign guest. When Wilde stepped onto the lecture platform of the Boston Music Hall, he faced sixty Harvard freshmen in the front two rows, all dressed alike in swallowtail coats, wigs, and green ties. Each had a large lily in his buttonhole, simpered over the sunflower he held, and applauded every time Wilde paused for a sip of water.

Oscar was ready for them, however. He wore conventional evening dress that night and got the audience on his side with the remark that he "seemed to see certain signs of an artistic movement in the lecture hall." His epigram "Caricature is the tribute mediocrity pays to genius" and his fervent prayer to be saved from his disciples brought the house down. At the end of the evening Harvard's score was zero.

The Harvard story aroused indignation in the West. People in longhorn country were shocked at the Boston Brahmins'[3] treatment of their visitor and decided to show Wilde true hospitality if he ever came their way. The chance came when Oscar agreed to give twenty lectures on the Pacific coast in March and April for sixty percent of the gross, a minimum guarantee of $200 a night paid in advance, and traveling expenses.

On the first day of spring Oscar lectured at the Social Art Club of Omaha on "Decorative Art," a field in which he found Americans decidedly deficient. Their houses were "illy designed, decorated shabbily, and in bad taste, filled with furniture that was not honestly made."

It was one hundred rattling train hours from Omaha to San Francisco. Oscar watched the gray prairies absorb time and space like "blotting paper." He composed an epitaph for Longfellow, whom he had visited in Boston ("Longfellow was himself a beautiful poem, more beautiful than anything he ever wrote"); complained to the newsboys selling pirated editions of his poems for ten cents that "though poets like to be popular they desire to be paid"; compared the heavy, awkward buffalo on the desolate plains to a certain English drama critic; and wrote home that he was "somewhere in the middle of coyotes and cañons: one is a 'ravine' and the other a 'fox,' I don't know which, but I think they change about."

Finally the train came down from the mountains into California's green fields, groves of orange trees, and purple

---

3. **Brahmin (brä′ min):** a cultured person from a long-established upper-class family.

hills, "a very Italy, without its art." Liking California better than any other part of America, Oscar was to lecture in San Jose, Sacramento, Oakland, and—on several occasions—San Francisco. He found her a "really beautiful city" and Chinatown "the most artistic city I have ever come across." He later said, "I used to watch a great hulking Chinese workman at his task of digging, and used to see him every day drink his tea from a little cup as delicate in texture as the petal of a flower, whereas in all the grand hotels of the land, where thousands of dollars have been lavished on great gilt mirrors and gaudy columns, I have been given my coffee or my chocolate in cups an inch and a quarter thick."

The "grand hotel" he stayed at in San Francisco was the Palace—a massive, block-long building with a glass-covered court open to carriages. It also had "rising rooms," that could carry a guest to any one of the hotel's seven stories. Although Oscar continued to wear the lecture costume his audience expected, offstage he simplified his dress and went "western" with a broad brimmed, white sombrero on top of his long hair. . . .

Wilde's first lecture in San Francisco, "The English Renaissance," attracted a fashionable audience in Platt's Hall. San Franciscans applauded his statement that "the value of the telephone is the value of what two people have to say" and his plea to give children beauty instead of the "record of bloody slaughters and barbarous brawls" called history or "of the latitude and longitude of places nobody cares to visit" called geography. In his second lecture, "House Decoration," he castigated the ugliness of machine-made furniture, cast-iron stoves, and pictures hung in hallways or too high to be seen. Taking the stage the third time, Oscar directed his audience to

hang pictures at eye level. "The habit in America of
hanging them up near the cornice struck me as irrational
at first. It was not until I saw how bad the pictures were
that I realized the advantage of the custom." The decoration of plates with sunsets and moonlight scenes also displeased the aesthete. "We do not want a soup plate whose
bottom seems to vanish in the distance," he said. "One
feels neither safe nor comfortable under such conditions."
The horsehair sofa was that old offender "whose stolid
look of indifference is always so depressing." Artists and
handicraftsmen, Oscar insisted, should work together to
produce beautiful and useful objects based on rational
design.

The *Sacramento Bee* kept close tabs on Wilde during his
stay in California. It expected the "aesthetic females" of
San Francisco to shower him with bouquets, advised the
Society for the Prevention of Dissemination of Obscene
Literature to look into some of his poetry, and printed the
following verse:

> O had I the limbs of Oscar Wilde
> I'd pose in the gleam of the lily flower—
> Or prance in public, a gushing child,
> And line with ducats my sylvan bower!

This was typical of the gibes American newspapers frequently directed at Wilde for having found a good thing
in aestheticism. When Oscar spoke on "Art Decoration"
in Sacramento, the *Bee* noted his monotonous delivery—
"never so much as recognizing a comma or a period but
going straight on in a drawling tone from beginning to
end." The reporter did, however, find the subject well prepared and the poet's language good. . . .

Oscar's entertainment varied. Once after lecturing, he was invited to a musical and literary evening for members of the Bric-a-Brac Club. Knowing what was expected of him, he turned out in ruffles and velvet to see the display of still lifes, hand-painted handkerchief boxes, and pencil studies of stags' heads.

There were livelier invitations too. The day before Oscar left San Francisco, he went to tea at the studio of painter Joe Strong and his wife Isobel, daughter of Robert Louis Stevenson's wife Fanny and her first husband. None of the artists in this Bohemian milieu had ever given a tea before, so the Strongs' Chinese servant came to the rescue with a tea service of delicate china arranged on a teakwood table. He wore a mandarin cap, tucked his hands into the sleeves of his brocaded gown, and he bowed at appropriate moments. The skylight had been painted over with clusters of red roses and green leaves for the occasion, and one of the ladies appeared in a long, black silk dress trimmed with lace. As he walked into the studio, Oscar exclaimed, "This is where I belong! This is my atmosphere! I didn't know such a place existed in the whole United States." San Francisco was Oscar's biggest success. And he left in his wake a trail of sunflower fans, hollyhock hats, petals appliqued on lace curtains, echoes of "utterly utter" and "too-too-excessively beyond" in Nob Hill[4] drawing rooms. . . .

Denver was next, and the bonanza city went agog over the visit of the famous aesthete. Tickets to his lecture in the Grand Opera House sold for one dollar and fifty cents instead of one dollar—the price having been raised to fit the audience's pocketbook. Oscar's hotel suite was done over for him with lilies and sunflowers on pink wallpaper,

---

4. **Nob Hill:** a prestigious San Francisco neighborhood.

a ceiling fresco, and a classical statuary in the bathroom.
Dry goods stores had Oscar Wilde patterns, and china
shops advertised "Oscar Wilde Majolica and Limoges."[5]

After Wilde's lecture which, it was said, "never
stirred his audience but in the direction of the door,"
Horace Tabor, multimillionaire silver king of Leadville,
invited the poet to visit Matchless Mine in the richest and
roughest city in the country. Wilde was warned, according to a story he liked to tell, that he or his traveling manager would be shot if they came to Leadville; to which he
replied that nothing they could do to his traveling manager
would intimidate him. In this mining town of clapboard
houses [and] bare cabins . . . Oscar lectured on "House
Decoration" clad in knee breeches and a velvet jacket.
His listeners were miners, the only well-dressed men in
America, Oscar insisted, because their shirts, kerchiefs,
corduroys, and high boots resembled those of Charles I's
cavaliers. Pleased by hearing parts of the autobiography
of Benvenuto Cellini[6] the miners asked why Oscar had
not brought Cellini with him. Wilde carefully explained
that the Florentine sculptor had been dead for a long
time; whereupon a voice from the audience demanded,
"Who shot him?"

Later the aesthete was given a night tour of Leadville.
In one saloon he noticed a sign above the piano: "Don't
shoot the pianist; he's doing his damndest." Wilde said
this was the only rational method of art criticism he had
ever come across. At 2:00 A.M., dressed in Tabor's own
underground rubber suit, Oscar descended Matchless
Mine in an ore bucket. At the bottom of the mine he sat
down to a banquet, "the first course of which was

---

5. **Majolica (mə jäl′ i kə) and Limoges (lē mōzh′):** a variety of Italian pottery
and a fine French porcelain.
6. **Benvenuto Cellini:** 1500–71; an Italian sculptor and goldsmith.

whiskey, the second whiskey, and the third the same."
The miners invited Wilde to open a new vein called "the
Oscar" with a silver drill, his only memento of the event.
He had hoped that "in their simple grand way" the miners
would offer him shares in it, but "in their artless untu-
tored fashion they did not."

Before leaving the state, Wilde lectured in Pueblo and
Colorado Springs. On his way east, he stopped in
Lincoln, Nebraska. When taken to see the prison there,
Oscar was consoled in his concern for the prisoners to
find that they were all mean looking. "I should hate to
see a criminal with a noble face," he said. In one "tragi-
cally tidy" whitewashed cell Oscar found a translation of
Dante and thought it "strange and beautiful" that the
exiled poet's sorrow should be the comfort of a prisoner
in a modern jail, hundreds of years later.

Oscar Wilde left America on December 27, 1882,
having arranged for a New York production of *Vera* the
following year. To his manager's request that he make
certain changes in the play, Wilde replied, "Who am I to
tamper with a masterpiece?" The years of glory when he
would be England's leading playwright lay ahead. The
years of shame and suffering when he himself would read
Dante in Reading Gaol[7] were not even conceivable.

■ ■ ■

---

7. Reading Gaol the jail in the south central English town of Reading where
Wilde was imprisoned from 1895 to 1897.

What is abnormal in Life stands in normal relations to Art. It is the only thing in Life that stands in normal relations to Art.

Oscar Wilde

The Days I Knew

Lillie Langtry (Lady De Bathe)

Vividly I recall the first meeting with Oscar Wilde in the studio of Frank Miles, and how astonished I was at his strange appearance. Then he must have been not more than twenty-two. He had a profusion of brown hair, brushed back from his forehead, and worn rather longer than was conventional, though not with the exaggeration which he afterwards affected. His face was large, and so colourless that a few pale freckles of good size were oddly conspicuous. He had a well-shaped mouth, with somewhat coarse lips and greenish-hued teeth. The plainness of his face, however was redeemed by the splendour of his great, eager eyes.

In height he was about six feet, and broad in proportion. His hands were large and indolent, with pointed fingers and perfectly-shaped filbert nails, indicative of his artistic disposition. The nails, I regretfully record, rarely received the attention they deserved. To me he was always grotesque in appearance, although I have seen him described by a French writer as "beautiful" and "Apollo-like." That he possessed a remarkably fascinating and compelling personality, and what in an actor would be termed wonderful "stage presence," is beyond question, and there was about him an enthusiasm singularly captivating. He had one of the most alluring voices that I have ever listened to, round and soft, and full of variety and expression, and the cleverness of his remarks received added value from his manner of delivering them.

His customary apparel consisted of light-coloured trousers, a black frock coat, only the lower button fastened, a brightly flowered waistcoat blossoming underneath, and a white silk cravat, held together by an old intaglio amethyst set as a pin. I do not think I ever met him wearing gloves, but he always carried a pale lavender pair, using them to give point to his gestures, which were many and varied. Apropos of his dress, I recall seeing him (after he had become celebrated and prosperous), at the first night of one of his plays, come before the curtain, in response to the applause of the audience, wearing a black velvet jacket, lavender trousers, and a variegated waistcoat, a white straw hat in one hand and a lighted cigarette in the other.

In the early part of our acquaintance Wilde was *really* ingenuous. His mannerisms and eccentricities were then but the natural outcome of a young fellow bubbling over with temperament, and were not at all assumed. Later, when he began to rise as a figure in the life of London, and his unconscious peculiarities had become a target for the humorous columns of the newspapers, he was quick to realise that they could be turned to advantage, and he proceeded forthwith to develop them so audaciously that it became impossible to ignore them.

He was ridiculed and he was imitated. When he wore a daisy in his buttonhole, thousands of young men did likewise. When he proclaimed the sunflower "adorable," it was to be found adorning every drawing-room. His edict that severely plain and flowering garments were the only becoming covering for the female form sent every young woman, and many elderly ones, scampering off to their *modistes* with delirious suggestions for Grecian draperies.

In the queer jargon of the day, he was the "Apostle of the Lily," the "Apostle of the Transcendental," and, among the revilers, the "Apostle of the Utterly-Utter and Too-Too." His affectations, I may say, were mainly for the benefit of the general public. To his friends he always remained the same, and both friends and enemies were forced to confess his brilliancy in spite of his shams. His vogue spread rapidly, and soon he was lionised by both artistic and social sets of London. It seemed to me, however, that he gradually grew less spontaneous and more laboured in his conversation as he became the fashion, which was not to be wondered at when he was counted on to be the life of every afternoon tea, and was expected to supply a *bon mot* between every mouthful at dinner.

His mother, Lady Wilde, lived a retired life in Onslow Square, sometimes emerging from her seclusion to give an afternoon at-home to guests invited by her two sons. On these occasions she used to pull down the blinds and light the lamps, even on summer days. She was a poetess, and wrote verses under the *nom de plume* of Esperanza, so perhaps her son partly inherited his poetic gift from his mother. Some said his elder brother, Willie, was as clever in his way, but I found him quite uninteresting.

When I met Oscar he had come down from Oxford fresh from winning the prize for the best poem of the year, called "Ravenna," but he was very modest about his success, and I heard the fact only from others. Presently, other and beautiful verses from his pen began to attract unusual attention and admiration, and it was then that I became the inspiration for one of his happiest efforts. The poem, which, with a dedication to me, originally appeared in *The World* (a society paper edited by Edmund Yates), is included in Oscar's first volume. He presented me with a white vellum-bound copy bearing the following charming inscription:

"To Helen, formerly of Troy, now of London."

Before Oscar had achieved celebrity, and was unconsciously on the verge of it, he always made a point of bringing me flowers, but he was not in circumstances to afford great posies, so, in coming to call, he would drop into Covent Garden flower market, buy me a single gorgeous amaryllis (all his slender purse would allow), and stroll down Piccadilly carefully carrying the solitary flower. The scribblers construed his act of homage as a pose, and thus I innocently conferred on him the title "Apostle of the Lily."

On my first visit to America he was likewise touring under Henry Abbey's management, and I was amused to find him "dressed for the part." He was wearing a black velvet suit with knickerbockers, silk stockings, and black shoes with silver buckles, his neck embellished by a Bryonic collar, and was lecturing on Greek art. Being asked by the U.S. Customs on his arrival the usual question: "Have you anything contraband?" he replied superbly, "No, I have nothing to declare but my genius." His success was only moderate, probably due to the fact that the press agent sought to impress the public with Oscar's personal eccentricities rather than with his genuine culture.

He was lecturing and I was playing at Buffalo at the same time that season, so we visited Niagara in a party, and in an interview he gave a reporter on his impressions of these mighty waters, he announced, "that Mrs. Langtry was photographed with Niagara Falls as an unpretentious background!" A year later, when I was presenting the play (adapted from Sardou's *Nos Intimes*) called *Peril* in the States, Oscar became engaged to a beautiful Irish girl, and he sent me the following letter announcing the fact:

> I am really delighted at your immense success; the most brilliant telegrams have appeared in the papers here on your performance in *Peril*. You have done what no other artist of your day has done, invaded America a second time and carried off new victories. But then, you are made for victory. It has always flashed in your eyes and rung in your voice.
>
> And so I write to tell you how glad I am at your triumphs—you,—Venus Victrix[1] of our age—and the

---

1. **Venus Victrix:** victorious Venus; in Greek mythology the goddess of love and beauty.

other half to tell you that I am going to be married to a beautiful girl called Constance Lloyd—a grave, slight, violet-eyed little Artemis,[2] with great coils of heavy brown hair which makes her flower-like head droop like a blossom, and wonderful ivory hands which draw music from the piano so sweet that the birds stop singing to listen to her. We are to be married in April. I hope so much that you will be over then. I am so anxious for you to know and like her.

I am hard at work lecturing and getting rich, though it is horrid being so much away from her, but we telegraph to each other twice a day, and I rush back suddenly from the uttermost parts of the earth to see her for an hour, and do all the foolish things that wise lovers do.

Will you write me and wish me all happiness, and Believe me,

Ever devoted and affectionate,

OSCAR WILDE.

Oscar's contemplated marriage did not surprise me, as I knew that he had for some time admired the girl who afterwards became his wife, and of whom he had often talked rapturously to me. I did not see him again for several years, as I remained in the States, and when we next met in London he had become a successful dramatist.

When his play *The Importance of Being Earnest* was in rehearsal at the St. James's everyone concerned was bound to secrecy by George Alexander. Oscar was adamant, and rather irritating one afternoon when I tried to worm the plot out of him. Next day he came to tea, and I thought I would get my own back, so I said: "Arthur Bourchier lunched here and told me all about it!" (He was playing an important part.) "Who else was there?" gasped Oscar.

---

2. **Artemis:** in Greek mythology the goddess of the woodlands and the moon.

I said casually, "Only Smalley." (Exit the author hurriedly, moaning.) Two hours later, enter A. B., almost crying with annoyance: "What's all this?" "Only my joke. I'll write to Alexander." I did, and got a freezing reply saying he "did not understand jokes in business." In the evening Tree[3] heard the story at the Garrick. "I am sure the Lily did that," he said.

■ ■ ■

---

3. **Herbert Beerbohm Tree:** an actor-manager at the Haymarket Theater; a friend to Wilde.

Art is the only serious thing in the world. And the artist is the only person who is never serious.

Oscar Wilde

To L. L.
Oscar Wilde

COULD we dig up this long-buried treasure,
    Were it worth pleasure,
We never could learn love's song,
    We are parted too long.

Could the passionate past that is fled
    Call back its dead,
Could we live it all over again,
    Were it worth the pain!

I remember we used to meet
    By an ivied seat,
And you warbled each pretty word
    With the air of a bird;

And your voice had a quaver in it,
    Just like a linnet,
And shook, as the blackbird's throat
    With its last big note;

And your eyes, they were green and grey
    Like an April day,
But lit into amethyst
    When I stooped and kissed;

And your mouth, it would never smile
    For a long, long while,
Then it rippled all over with laughter
    Five minutes after.

You were always afraid of a shower
    Just like a flower:
I remember you started and ran
    When the rain began.

I remember I never could catch you,
    For no one could match you,
You had wonderful, luminous, fleet,
    Little wings to your feet.

I remember your hair—did I tie it?
    For it always ran riot—
Like a tangled sunbeam of gold:
    These things are old.

I remember so well the room,
    And the lilac bloom
That beat at the dripping pane
    In the warm June rain;

And the colour of your gown,
    It was amber-brown,
And two yellow satin bows
    From your shoulders rose.

And the handkerchief of French lace
    Which you held to your face—
Had a small tear left a stain?
    Or was it the rain?

On your hand as it waved adieu
    There were veins of blue;
In your voice as it said good-bye
    Was a petulant cry,

"You have only wasted your life."
   (Ah, that was the knife!)
When I rushed through the garden gate
   It was all too late.

Could we live it over again,
   Were it worth the pain,
Could the passionate past that is fled
   Call back its dead!

Well if my heart must break,
   Dear love, for your sake,
It will break in music, I know,
   Poets' hearts break so.

But strange that I was not told
   That the brain can hold
In a tiny ivory cell
   God's heaven and hell.

■ ■ ■

*It is a very sad thing that
nowadays there is so little
useless information.*

Oscar Wilde

The Naming of Cats
T. S. Eliot

The Naming of Cats is a difficult matter,
    It isn't just one of your holiday games;
You may think at first I'm as mad as a hatter
When I tell you, a cat must have THREE DIFFERENT NAMES.
First of all, there's the name that the family use daily,
    Such as Peter, Augustus, Alonzo or James,
Such as Victor or Jonathan, George or Bill Bailey—
    All of them sensible everyday names.
There are fancier names if you think they sound sweeter,
    Some for the gentlemen, some for the dames:
Such as Plato, Admetus, Electra, Demeter—
    But all of them sensible everyday names.
But I tell you, a cat needs a name that's particular,
    A name that's peculiar, and more dignified,
Else how can he keep up his tail perpendicular,
    Or spread out his whiskers, or cherish his pride?
Of names of this kind, I can give you a quorum
    Such as Munkustrap, Quaxo, or Coricopat,
Such as Bombalurina, or else Jellylorum—
    Names that never belong to more than one cat.
But above and beyond there's still one name left over,
    And that is the name that you never will guess;
The name that no human research can discover—
    But THE CAT HIMSELF KNOWS, and will never confess.
When you notice a cat in profound meditation,

The reason, I tell you, is always the same:
His mind is engaged in a rapt contemplation
Of the thought, of the thought, of the thought of his
name:
His ineffable effable
Effanineffable
Deep and inscrutable singular Name.

■ ■ ■

Education is an admirable thing. But it is well to remember from time to time that nothing that is worth knowing can be taught.

Oscar Wilde

My Name

Sandra Cisneros

In English my name means hope. In Spanish it means too many letters. It means sadness, it means waiting. It is like the number nine. A muddy color. It is the Mexican records my father plays on Sunday mornings when he is shaving, songs like sobbing.

It was my great-grandmother's name and now it is mine. She was a horse woman too, born like me in the Chinese year of the horse—which is supposed to be bad luck if you're born female—but I think this is a Chinese lie because the Chinese, like the Mexicans, don't like their women strong.

My great-grandmother. I would've liked to have known her, a wild horse of a woman, so wild she wouldn't marry. Until my great-grandfather threw a sack over her head and carried her off. Just like that, as if she were a fancy chandelier. That's the way he did it.

And the story goes she never forgave him. She looked out the window her whole life; the way so many women sit their sadness on an elbow. I wonder if she made the best with what she got or was she sorry because she couldn't be all the things she wanted to be. Esperanza. I have inherited her name, but I don't want to inherit her place by the window.

At school they say my name funny as if the syllables were made out of tin and hurt the roof of your mouth. But in Spanish my name is made out of a softer something, like silver, not quite as thick as sister's name—Magdalena—which is uglier than mine. Magdalena who at least can come home and become Nenny. But I am always Esperanza.

I would like to baptize myself under a new name, a name more like the real me, the one nobody sees. Esperanza as Lisandra or Maritza or Zeze the X. Yes. something like Zeze the X will do.

And Some More

Sandra Cisneros

The Eskimos got thirty different names for snow, I say. I read it in a book.

I got a cousin, Rachel says, she got three different names.

There ain't thirty different kinds of snow, Lucy says. There are two kinds. The clean kind and the dirty kind, clean and dirty. Only two.

There are a million zillion kinds, says Nenny, no two exactly alike. Only how do you remember which one is which?

She got three last names and, let me see, two first names. One in English and one in Spanish . . .

And clouds got at least ten different names, I say.

Names for clouds? Nenny asks, names just like you and me?

That up there, that's cumulus, and everybody looks up.

Cumulus are cute, Rachel says. She would say something like that.

What's that one there? Nenny asks, pointing a finger.

That's cumulus too. They're all cumulus today. Cumulus, cumulus, cumulus.

No, she says. That there is Nancy, otherwise known as Pig-eye. And over there her cousin Mildred, and little Joey, Marco, Nereida and Sue.

There are all different kinds of clouds. How many different kinds of clouds can you think of?

Well, there's these already that look like shaving cream . . .

And what about the kind that looks like you combed its hair? Yes, those are clouds too.

Phyllis, Ted, Alfredo and Julie . . .

There are clouds that look like big fields of sheep, Rachel says. Them are my favorite.

And don't forget nimbus the rain cloud, I add, that's something.

Jose and Dagoberto, Alicia, Raul, Edna, Alma and Rickey . . .

There's that wide puffy cloud that looks like your face when you wake up after falling asleep with all your clothes on.

Reynaldo, Angelo, Albert, Armando, Mario . . .

Not my face. Looks like your fat face.

Rita, Margie, Ernie . . .

Whose fat face?

Esperanza's fat face, that's who. Looks like Esperanza's ugly face when she comes to school in the morning.

Anita, Stella, Dennis, and Lolo . . .

Who you calling ugly, ugly?

Richie, Yolanda, Hector, Stevie, Vincent . . .

Not you. Your mama, that's who.

My mama? You better not be saying that, Lucy Guerrero. You better not be talking like that . . . else you can say goodbye to being my friend forever.

I'm saying your mama's ugly like . . . ummm . . .

. . . like bare feet in September!

That does it! Both of yous better get out of my yard before I call my brothers.

Oh, we're only playing.

I can think of thirty Eskimo words for you, Rachel. Thirty words that say what you are.

Oh yeah, well I can think of some more.

Uh-oh, Nenny. Better get the broom. Too much trash in our yard today.

Frankie, Licha, Maria, Pee Wee . . .

Nenny, you better tell your sister she is really crazy because Lucy and me are never coming back here again. Forever.

Reggie, Elizabeth, Lisa, Louie . . .

You can do what you want to do, Nenny, but you better not talk to Lucy or Rachel if you want to be my sister.

You know what you are, Esperanza? You are like the Cream of Wheat cereal. You're like the lumps.

Yeah, and you're foot fleas, that's you.

Chicken lips.

Rosemary, Dalia, Lily . . .

Cockroach jelly.

Jean, Geranium and Joe . . .

Cold *frijoles.*

Mimi, Michael, Moe . . .

Your mama's *frijoles.*

Your ugly mama's toes.

That's stupid.

Bebe, Blana, Benny . . .

Who's stupid?

Rachel, Lucy, Esperanza, and Nenny.

■ ■ ■

The only thing that can console one for being poor is extravagance. The only thing that can console one for being rich is economy.

Oscar Wilde

the endless streetcar ride into the night, and the tinfoil noose

Jean Shepherd

*There are about four times in a man's life, or a woman's,
too . . . when unexpectedly, from out of the darkness
. . . the cosmic searchlight of Truth shines full upon them.*

Mewling, puking babes. That's the way we all start.
Damply clinging to someone's shoulder, burping weakly,
clawing our way into life. *All* of us. Then gradually, surely,
we begin to divide into two streams, all marching together
up that long yellow brick road of life, but on opposite
sides of the street. One crowd goes on to become the
Official people, peering out at us from television screens,
magazine covers. They are forever appearing in newsreels,
carrying attaché cases, surrounded by banks of micro-
phones while the world waits for their decisions and state-
ments. And the rest of us go on to become . . . just us.

They are the Prime Ministers, the Presidents, Cabinet
members, Stars, dynamic molders of the Universe, while
we remain forever the onlookers, the applauders of their
real lives.

Forever down in the dark dungeons of our souls we
ask ourselves:

"How did they get away from me? When did I make
that first misstep that took me forever to the wrong side
of the street, to become eternally part of the accursed,
anonymous Audience?"

It seems like one minute we're all playing around
back of the garage, kicking tin cans and yelling at girls,
and the next instant you find yourself doomed to exist as
an office boy in the Mail Room of Life, while another

ex-mewling, puking babe sends down Dicta, says "No comment" to the Press, and lives a real, genuine *Life* on the screen of the world.

Countless sufferers at this hour are spending billions of dollars and endless man-hours lying on analysts' couches, trying to pinpoint the exact moment that they stepped off the track and into the bushes forever.

It all hinges on one sinister reality that is rarely mentioned, no doubt due to its implacable, irreversible inevitability. These decisions cannot be changed, no matter how many brightly cheerful, buoyantly optimistic books on HOW TO ACHIEVE A RICHER, FULLER, MORE BOUNTIFUL LIFE or SEVEN MAGIC GOLDEN KEYS TO INSTANT DYNAMIC SUCCESS or THE SECRET OF HOW TO BECOME A BILLIONAIRE we read, or how many classes are attended for instruction in hand-shaking, back-slapping, grinning, and making After-Dinner speeches, Joseph Stalin was not a Dale Carnegie graduate.[1] He went all the way. It is an unpleasant truth that is swallowed, if at all, like a rancid, bitter pill. A star is a star; a numberless cipher is a numberless cipher.

Even more eerie a fact is that the Great Divide is rarely a matter of talent or personality. Or even luck. Adolf Hitler had a notoriously weak handshake. His smile was, if anything, a vapid mockery. But inevitably his star zoomed higher and higher. Cinema luminaries of the first order are rarely blessed with even the modicum of Talent, and often their physical beauty leaves much to be desired. What is the difference between Us and Them, We and They, the Big Ones and the great, teeming rabble?

There are about four times in a man's life, or a woman's, too, for that matter, when unexpectedly, from out of the darkness, the blazing carbon lamp, the cosmic

---

1. "Joseph Stalin . . . graduate.": Stalin was the premier of the U.S.S.R. from 1941 to 1953. The Dale Carnegie course teaches the adoption of certain positive attitudes as aids to successful living.

searchlight of Truth shines full upon them. It is how we react to those moments that forever seals our fate. One crowd simply puts on its sunglasses, lights another cigar, and heads for the nearest plush French restaurant in the jazziest section of town, sits down and orders a drink, and ignores the whole thing. While we, the Doomed, caught in the brilliant glare of illumination, see ourselves inescapably for what we are, and from that day on skulk in the weeds, hoping no one else will spot us.

Those moments happen when we are least able to fend them off. I caught the first one full in the face when I was fourteen. The fourteenth summer is a magic one for all kids. You have just slid out of the pupa stage, leaving your old baby skin behind, and have not yet become a grizzled, hardened, tax-paying beetle. At fourteen you are made of cellophane. You curl easily and everyone can see through you.

When I was fourteen, life was flowing through me in a deep, rich torrent of Castoria. How did I know that the first rocks were just ahead, and I was about to have my keel ripped out on the reef? Sometimes you feel as though you are alone in a rented rowboat, bailing like mad in the darkness with a leaky bailing can. It is important to know that there are at least two billion other ciphers in the same boat, bailing with the same leaky can. They all think they are alone and are crossed with an evil star. They are right.

I'm fourteen years old, in my sophomore year at high school. One day Schwartz, my purported best friend, sidled up to me edgily outside of school while we were waiting on the steps to come in after lunch. He proceeded to outline his plan:

"Helen's old man won't let me take her out on a date on Saturday night unless I get a date for her girlfriend. A double date. The old coot figures, I guess, that if there are four of us there won't be no monkey business. Well, how about it? Do you want to go on a blind date with this chick? I never seen her."

Well. For years I had this principle—absolutely *no* blind dates. I was a man of perception and taste, and life was short. But there is a time in your life when you have to stop taking and begin to give just a little. For the first time the warmth of sweet Human Charity brought the roses to my cheeks. After all Schwartz was my friend. It was little enough to do, have a blind date with some no doubt skinny, pimply girl for your best friend. I would do it for Schwartz. He would do as much for me.

"Okay. Okay, Schwartz."

Then followed the usual ribald remarks, feckless boasting, and dirty jokes about dates in general and girls in particular. It was decided that next Saturday we would go. . . . I had a morning paper route at the time and my life savings stood at about $1.80. I was all set to blow it on one big night.

I will never forget that particular Saturday as long as I live. The air was as soft as the finest of spun silk. The scent of lilacs hung heavy. The catalpa trees rustled in the early evening breeze from off the Lake. . . .

All that afternoon I had carefully gone over my wardrobe to select the proper symphony of sartorial brilliance. That night I set out wearing my magnificent electric blue sport coat, whose shoulders were so wide that they hung out over my frame like vast, drooping eaves, so wide I had difficulty going through an ordinary door head-on. The electric blue sport coat that draped voluminously almost to my knees, its wide lapels flapping soundlessly in the slightest breeze. My pleated gray flannel slacks began just below my breastbone and indeed chafed my armpits. High-belted, cascading down finally to grasp my ankles in a vice-like grip. My tie, indeed one of my most prized possessions, had been a gift from my Aunt Glenn upon the state occasion of graduation from eighth grade. It was of a beautiful silky fabric, silvery pearly colored, four inches wide at the fulcrum, and of such a length to endanger occasionally my zipper in moments of haste. Hand-painted upon it was a magnificent blood-red snail.

I had spent fully two hours carefully arranging and rearranging my great mop of wavy hair, into which I had rubbed fully a pound and a half of Greasy Kid Stuff.

Helen and Schwartz waited on the corner under the streetlight at the streetcar stop near Junie Jo's home. Her name was Junie Jo Prewitt. I won't soon forget it quickly, although she has, no doubt, forgotten mine. I walked down the dark street alone, past houses set back off the street, through the darkness, past privet hedges, under elm trees, through air rich and ripe with promise. Her house stood back from the street even farther than the others. It sort of crouched in the darkness, looking out at me, kneeling. Pregnant with Girldom. A real Girlfriend house.

The first faint touch of nervousness filtered through the marrow of my skullbone as I knocked on the door of the screen-enclosed porch. No answer. I knocked again, louder. Through the murky screens I could see faint lights in the house itself. Still no answer. Then I found a small doorbell button buried in the sash. I pressed. From far off in the bowels of the house I heard two chimes "Bong" politely. It sure didn't sound like our doorbell. We had a real ripper that went off like a broken buzz saw, more of a BRRRAAAAKKK than a muffled Bong. This was a rich people's doorbell.

The door opened and there stood a real, genuine, gold-plated Father: potbelly, underwear shirt, suspenders, and all.

"Well?" he asked.

For one blinding moment of embarrassment I couldn't remember her name. After all, she was a blind date. I couldn't just say:

"I'm here to pick up some girl."

He turned back into the house and hollered:

"JUNIE JO! SOME KID'S HERE!"

"Heh, heh. . . ." I countered.

He led me into the living room. It was an itchy house, sticky stucco walls of a dull orange color, and all over the floor this Oriental rug with the design crawling around, making loops and sworls. I sat on an overstuffed chair covered in stiff green mohair that scratched even through my slacks. Little twisty bridge lamps stood everywhere. I instantly began to sweat down the back of my clean white shirt. Like I said, it was a very itchy house. It had little lamps sticking out of the walls that looked like phony candles, with phony glass orange flames. The rug started moaning to itself.

I sat on the edge of the chair and tried to talk to this Father. He was a Cub fan. We struggled under water for what seemed like an hour and a half, when suddenly I heard someone coming down the stairs. First the feet; then those legs, and there she was. She was magnificent! The greatest-looking girl I ever saw in my life! I have hit the double jackpot! And on a blind date! Great Scot!

My senses actually reeled as I clutched the arm of that bilge-green chair for support. Junie Jo Prewitt made Cleopatra look like a Girl Scout.

Five minutes later we are sitting in the streetcar, heading toward the bowling alley. I am sitting next to the most fantastic creation in the Feminine department known to Western man. There are the four of us in that long, yellow-lit streetcar. No one else was aboard; just us four. I, naturally, being a trained gentleman, sat on the aisle to protect her from candy wrappers and cigar butts and such. Directly ahead of me, also on the aisle, sat Schwartz, his arm already flung affectionately in a death grip around Helen's neck as we boomed and rattled through the night.

I casually flung my right foot up onto my left knee so that she could see my crepe-soled, perforated, wing-toed, Scotch bluchers with the two-toned laces. I started to work my famous charm on her. Casually, with my practiced offhand, cynical, cutting, sardonic humor I told her about how my Old Man had cracked the block in the Oldsmobile, how the White Sox were going to have a good year this year, how my kid brother wet his pants when he saw a snake, how I figured it was going to rain, what a great guy Schwartz was, what a good second baseman I was, how I figured I might go out for football. On and on I rolled, like Old Man River, pausing significantly for her to pick up the conversation. Nothing.

Ahead of us Schwartz and Helen were almost indistinguishable one from the other. They giggled, bit each other's ears, whispered, clasped hands, and in general made me itch even more.

From time to time Junie Jo would bend forward stiffly from the waist and say something I could never quite catch into Helen's right ear.

I told her my great story of the time that Uncle Carl lost his false teeth down the airshaft. Still nothing. Out of the corner of my eye I could see that she had her coat collar turned up, hiding most of her face as she sat silently, looking forward past Helen Weathers into nothingness.

I told her about this old lady on my paper route who chews tobacco and roller-skates in the backyard every morning. I still couldn't get through to her. Casually I inched my right arm up over the back of the seat behind her shoulders. The acid test. She leaned forward, avoiding my arm, and stayed that way.

"Heh, heh, heh. . . ."

As nonchalantly as I could, I retrieved it, battling a giant cramp in my right shoulder blade. I sat in silence for a few seconds, sweating heavily as ahead Schwartz and Helen are going at it hot and heavy.

It was then that I became aware of someone saying something to me. It was an empty car. There was no one else but us. I glanced around, and there it was. Above us a line of car cards looked down on the empty streetcar. One was speaking directly to me, to me alone.

DO YOU OFFEND?

Do I *offend?!*

With no warning, from up near the front of the car where the motorman is steering I see this thing coming down the aisle directly toward *me*. It's coming closer and closer. I can't escape it. It's this blinding, fantastic, brilliant, screaming blue light. I am spread-eagled in it. There's a pin sticking through my thorax. I see it all now.

I AM THE BLIND DATE!

ME!!

I'M the one they're being nice to!

I'm suddenly getting fatter, more itchy. My new shoes are like bowling balls with laces; thick, rubber-crepe bowling balls. My great tie that Aunt Glenn gave me is two feet wide, hanging down to the floor like some crinkly tinfoil noose. My beautiful hand-painted snail is seven feet high, sitting up on my shoulder, burping. Great Scot! It is all clear to me in the searing white light of Truth. My friend Schwartz, I can see him saying to Junie Jo:

"I got this crummy fat friend who never has a date. Let's give him a break and . . ."

I AM THE BLIND DATE!

They are being nice to *me!* She is the one who is out on a Blind Date. A Blind Date that didn't make it.

In the seat ahead, the merriment rose to a crescendo. Helen tittered; Schwartz cackled. The marble statue next to me stared gloomily out into the darkness as our street-car rattled on. The ride went on and on.

I AM THE BLIND DATE!

I didn't say much the rest of the night. There wasn't much to be said.

■ ■ ■

The only thing that the artist cannot see is the obvious. The only thing that the public can see is the obvious. . . .

Oscar Wilde

The Nightingale and the Rose

Oscar Wilde

"She said that she would dance with me if I brought her red roses," cried the young Student; "but in all my garden there is no red rose."

From her nest in the holm-oak tree the Nightingale heard him, and she looked out through the leaves, and wondered.

"No red rose in all my garden!" he cried, and his beautiful eyes filled with tears. "Ah, on what little things does happiness depend! I have read all that the wise men have written, and all the secrets of philosophy are mine, yet for want of a red rose is my life made wretched."

"Here at last is a true lover," said the Nightingale. "Night after night I have sung of him, though I knew him not: night after night have I told his story to the stars, and now I see him. His hair is dark as the hyacinth-blossom, and his lips are red as the rose of his desire; but passion has made his face like pale ivory, and sorrow has set her seal upon his brow."

"The Prince gives a ball to-morrow night," murmured the young Student, "and my love will be of the company. If I bring her a red rose she will dance with me till dawn. If I bring her a red rose, I shall hold her in my arms, and she will lean her head upon my shoulder, and her hand will be clasped in mine. But there is no red rose in my garden, so I shall sit lonely, and she will pass me by. She will have no heed of me, and my heart will break."

"Here indeed is the true lover," said the Nightingale. "What I sing of, he suffers; what is joy to me, to him is pain. Surely Love is a wonderful thing. It is more precious than emeralds, and dearer than fine opals. Pearls and pomegranates cannot buy it, nor is it set forth in the market-place. It may not be purchased of the merchants, nor can it be weighed out in the balance for gold."

"The musicians will sit in their gallery," said the young Student, "and play upon their stringed instruments, and my love will dance to the sound of the harp and the violin. She will dance so lightly that her feet will not touch the floor, and the courtiers in their gay dresses will throng round her. But with me she will not dance, for I have no red rose to give her;" and he flung himself down on the grass, and buried his face in his hands, and wept.

"Why is he weeping?" asked a little Green Lizard as he ran past him with his tail in the air.

"Why, indeed?" said a Butterfly, who was fluttering about after a sunbeam.

"Why, indeed?" whispered a Daisy to his neighbour, in a soft, low voice.

"He is weeping for a red rose," said the Nightingale.

"For a red rose!" they cried: "how very ridiculous!" and the little Lizard, who was something of a cynic, laughed outright.

But the Nightingale understood the secret of the Student's sorrow, and she sat silent in the Oak-tree, and thought about the mystery of Love.

Suddenly she spread her brown wings for flight, and soared into the air. She passed through the grove like a shadow, and like a shadow she sailed across the garden.

In the centre of the grass-plot was standing a beautiful Rose-tree, and when she saw it, she flew over to it, and lit upon a spray.

"Give me a red rose," she cried, "and I will sing you my sweetest song."

But the Tree shook its head.

"My roses are white," it answered; "as white as the foam of the sea, and whiter than the snow upon the mountain. But go to my brother who grows round the old sun-dial, and perhaps he will give you what you want."

So the Nightingale flew over to the Rose-tree that was growing round the old sun-dial.

"Give me a red rose," she cried, "and I will sing you my sweetest song."

But the Tree shook its head.

"My roses are yellow," it answered; "as yellow as the hair of the mermaiden who sits upon an amber throne, and yellower than the daffodil that blooms in the meadow before the mower comes with his scythe. But go to my brother who grows beneath the Student's window, and perhaps he will give you what you want."

So the Nightingale flew over to the Rose-tree that was growing beneath the Student's window.

"Give me a red rose," she cried, "and I will sing you my sweetest song."

But the Tree shook its head.

"My roses are red," it answered; "as red as the feet of the dove, and redder than the great fans of coral that wave and wave in the ocean cavern. But the winter has chilled my veins, and the frost has nipped my buds, and the storm has broken my branches, and I shall have no roses at all this year."

"One red rose is all I want," cried the Nightingale. "Only one red rose!" Is there any way by which I can get it?"

There is a way," answered the Tree; "but it is so terrible, that I dare not tell it to you."

"Tell it to me," said the Nightingale, "I am not afraid."

"If you want a red rose," said the Tree, "you must build it out of music by moonlight, and stain it with your own heart's-blood. You must sing to me with your breast against a thorn. All night long you must sing to me, and the thorn must pierce your heart, and your life-blood must flow into my veins, and become mine."

"Death is a great price to pay for a red rose," cried the Nightingale, "and Life is very dear to all. It is pleasant to sit in the green wood, and to watch the Sun in his chariot of gold, and the Moon in her chariot of pearl. Sweet is the scent of the hawthorn, and sweet are the bluebells that hide in the valley, and the heather that blows on the hill. Yet Love is better than Life, and what is the heart of a bird compared to the heart of a man?"

So she spread her wings for flight, and soared into the air. She swept over the garden like a shadow, and like a shadow she sailed through the grove.

The young Student was still lying on the grass, where she had left him, and the tears were not yet dry in his beautiful eyes.

"Be happy," cried the Nightingale, "be happy; you shall have your red rose. I will build it out of music by the moonlight, and stain it with my own heart's-blood. All that I ask of you in return is that you be a true lover, for Love is wiser than Philosophy, though she is wise, and mightier than Power, though he is mighty. Flame-coloured are his wings, and coloured like flame is his body. His lips are sweet as honey, and his breath is like frankincense."

The Student looked up from the grass, and listened, but he could not understand what the Nightingale was saying to him, for he only knew the things that are written down in books.

But the Oak-tree understood, and felt sad, for he was very fond of the little Nightingale who had built her nest in his branches.

"Sing me one last song," he whispered; "I shall feel very lonely when you are gone."

So the Nightingale sang to the Oak-tree, and her voice was like water bubbling from a silver jar.

When she had finished her song the Student got up, and pulled a note-book and a lead-pencil out of his pocket.

"She has form," he said to himself, as he walked away through the grove—"that cannot be denied her; but has she got feeling? I am afraid not. In fact, she is like most artists; she is all style, without any sincerity. She would not sacrifice herself for others. She thinks merely of music, and everybody knows that the arts are selfish. Still, it must be admitted that she has some beautiful notes in her voice. What a pity it is that they do not mean anything, or do any practical good." And he went into his room, and lay down on his little pallet-bed, and began to think of his love; and, after a time, he fell asleep.

And when the moon shone in the heavens the Nightingale flew to the Rose-tree, and set her breast against the thorn. All night she sang with her breast against the thorn, and the cold crystal Moon leaned down and listened. All night long she sang, and the thorn went deeper and deeper into her breast, and her life-blood ebbed away from her.

She sang first of the birth of love in the heart of a boy and a girl. And on the topmost spray of the Rose-tree there blossomed a marvellous rose, petal followed petal, as song followed song. Pale was it, at first, as the mist that hangs over the river—pale as the feet of the morning, and silver as the wings of the dawn. As the shadow of

a rose in a mirror of silver, as the shadow of a rose in a
water-pool, so was the rose that blossomed on the topmost spray of the Tree.

But the Tree cried to the Nightingale to press closer
against the thorn. "Press closer, little Nightingale," cried
the Tree, "or the Day will come before the rose is finished."

So the Nightingale pressed closer against the thorn,
and louder and louder grew her song, for she sang of the
birth of passion in the soul of a man and a maid.

And a delicate flush of pink came into the leaves of
the rose, like the flush in the face of the bride-groom
when he kisses the lips of the bride. But the thorn had not
yet reached her heart, so the rose's heart remained white,
for only a Nightingale's heart's-blood can crimson the
heart of a rose.

And the Tree cried to the Nightingale to press closer
against the thorn. "Press closer, little Nightingale," cried
the Tree, "or the Day will come before the rose is finished."

So the Nightingale pressed closer against the thorn
and the thorn touched her heart, and a fierce pang of pain
shot through her. Bitter, bitter was the pain, and wilder
and wilder grew her song, for she sang of the Love that
is perfected by Death, of the Love that dies not in the
tomb.

And the marvellous rose became crimson, like the
rose of the Eastern sky. Crimson was the girdle of petals,
and crimson as a ruby was the heart.

But the Nightingale's voice grew fainter, and her little
wings began to beat, and a film came over her eyes.
Fainter and fainter grew her song, and she felt something
choking her in her throat.

Then she gave one last burst of music. The white
Moon heard it, and she forgot the dawn, and lingered on

in the sky. The red rose heard it, and it trembled all over with ecstasy, and opened its petals to the cold morning air. Echo[1] bore it to her purple cavern in the hills, and woke the sleeping shepherds from their dreams. It floated through the reeds of the river, and they carried its message to the sea.

"Look, look!" cried the Tree, "the rose is finished now;" but the Nightingale made no answer, for she was lying dead in the long grass, with the thorn in her heart.

And at noon the Student opened his window and looked out.

"Why, what a wonderful piece of luck!" he cried; "here a red rose! I have never seen any rose like it in all my life. It is so beautiful that I am sure it has a long Latin name;" and he leaned down and plucked it.

Then he put on his hat, and ran up to the Professor's house with the rose in his hand.

The daughter of the Professor was sitting in the doorway winding blue silk on a reel, and her little dog was lying at her feet.

"You said you would dance with me if I brought you a red rose," cried the Student. "Here is the reddest rose in all the world. You will wear it to-night next to your heart, and as we dance together it will tell you how I love you."

But the girl frowned.

"I am afraid it will not go with my dress," she answered; "and, besides, the Chamberlain's nephew has sent me some real jewels, and everybody knows that jewels cost far more than flowers."

---

1. **Echo:** in Greek mythology a nymph cursed by Hera with the inability to speak except to repeat the last words said by another. Her passionate, yet unrequited, love for Narcissus made her fade away until all that remained of her was her voice.

"Well, upon my word, you are very ungrateful," said the Student angrily; and he threw the rose into the street, where it fell into the gutter, and a cart-wheel went over it.

"Ungrateful!" said the girl. "I tell you what, you are very rude; and after all, who are you? Only a Student. Why, I don't believe you have even got silver buckles on your shoes as the Chamberlain's nephew has;" and she got up from her chair and went into the house.

What a silly thing Love is," said the Student as he walked away. "It is not half as useful as Logic, for it does not prove anything, and it is always telling one of things that are not going to happen, and making one believe things that are not true. In fact, it is quite unpractical, and, as in this age to be practical is everything, I shall go back to Philosophy and study Metaphysics.

So he returned to his room and pulled out a great dusty book, and began to read.

■ ■ ■

*Public opinion exists only
where there are no ideas.*
                    Oscar Wilde

Oscar Wilde
(1854–1900)

Oscar Wilde was born in Dublin, Ireland. His father was a celebrated surgeon and his mother a poet. Wilde was an outstanding student of classical literature at Trinity College in Dublin and later at Oxford University. After touring Greece and Italy, Wilde lived in London, where he traveled in the social world of artists and intellectuals. He championed the cause of Aestheticism, a movement critical of the commercialism of the time. Wilde's motto was "Art for art's sake."

Wilde then lived for a while in Paris, leading the bohemian life while studying painting and literature. Returning to London, he married Constance Lloyd in 1884 and set up a fashionable home. Wilde wrote fairy tales for his two sons, book reviews, and essays. In 1891 he published his famous novel *The Picture of Dorian Gray*.

Needing money to support his extravagances, Wilde turned to the theater. His first play produced in London was the sentimental comedy *Lady Windermere's Fan* (1892), a problem play about a "woman with a past." Wilde wrote three more plays using similar ingredients: *A Woman of No Importance* (1893), *An Ideal Husband* (1894), and *The Importance of Being Earnest* (1895), which you are about to read. Wilde peppers the dialogue of all these plays with fresh, impertinent, and witty lines.

In 1895 Wilde was sentenced to two years in prison for immoral conduct, and *The Importance of Being Earnest* was closed at the height of its success, though it has been revived many times since then. After his release from prison, Wilde lived in France, where he died, deserted by most of his friends, in a Paris hotel in 1900.